American Vocabulary Program 1

John Flower

with

Michael Berman
Mark Powell
and
Ron Martínez

THOMSON

HEINLE

Australia Canada Mexico Singapore Spain United Kingdom United States

American Vocabulary Program 1
Lower Intermediate
Flower, Berman, Powell, Martínez

Publisher/Global ELT: *Christopher Wenger*
Executive Marketing Manager, Global ELT/ESL: *Amy Mabley*

Printed in Croatia by Zrinski d.d.
1 2 3 4 5 6 7 8 9 10   06 05 04 03 02

For more information contact Heinle, 25 Thomson Place, Boston, MA 02210 USA,
or you can visit our Internet site at http://www.heinle.com

For permission to use material from this text or product contact us:
Tel   1-800-730-2214
Fax   1-800-730-2215
Web   www.thomsonrights.com

ISBN: 0 906717 67 1

The Authors

John Flower
John Flower is a teacher at Eurocentre Bournemouth, where he has worked for many years. He has long experience of teaching students at all levels and has prepared many students for the Cambridge examinations. Her is the author of *First Certificate Organiser*, *Phrasal Verb Organiser*, and *Build Your Business Vocabulary*.

Ron Martínez
Ron is a native of California and has worked extensively as an ESL instructor in San Francisco, Los Angeles and Valencia, Spain. He is currently teaching at West Virginia University. He is responsible for this American edition.

Personal Note
The author would like to express his thanks to Michael Lewis for his enthusiasm and guidance, to Michael Berman who contributed some lively ideas for alternative ways to build vocabulary, and to Mark Powell for some more lexical exercises for this new edition. He would also like to thank his colleagues and students for their help, his wife for her typing and advice, and his children for not making too much noise!

Acknowledgements
Cover design Anna Macleod
Illustrations by James Slater
Ideas for illustrations from Argos.

Contents

Read this before you start

So you plan to build your vocabulary! Learning vocabulary is a very important part of learning English. If you make a grammar mistake, it may be "wrong" but very often people will understand you anyway. But if you don't know the exact word that you need, it is very frustrating for you, and the person you are talking to. Good English means having a big vocabulary!

There are better and worse ways to build your vocabulary and this book will help you to build your vocabulary quickly and effectively.
You will find it is best to work:

● systematically
● regularly
● personally

Don't just make lists of all the new words you encounter — plan and choose. Think of areas **you** are interested in; look for things **you** can't say in English, then fill those gaps in **your** vocabulary.

Don't do ten pages one day then nothing for three weeks! Try to do one or two pages every day. Regular work will help you to build effectively.

Don't just learn words; you also need to know how to use them. Which words does a word often combine with? This book will help you to learn more words, but also how to use the words you know more effectively. That is an important part of building your vocabulary.

Don't just use your dictionary when you have a problem. It is an important resource. It can help you in lots of different ways. There are tips all through this book to help you use your dictionary effectively.

Don't just make lists of new words; organize them. Again, there are tips to help you to learn and remember more of what you study.

Finally, there are a lot of words in English. Building your vocabulary is a long job! There are two more books in this series to help you learn more words, and to help you to enjoy the job!

1 Using a dictionary

If you want to learn English vocabulary, you should have a good English-English dictionary.

Use one with explanations that are easy to understand and which has sentences showing how you use the words.

Here are some questions to give you practice in using a dictionary.

A. Alphabetical order

Put these words into alphabetical order.

| car | action | accent | actor | card |
| about | carrot | act | active | above |

1. . . . .   6. . . . .
2. . . . .   7. . . . .
3. . . . .   8. . . . .
4. . . . .   9. . . . .
5. . . . .   10. . . . .

B. Meaning

Which of these do you usually find on a teapot?

| lake | lamb | leaf | lid | loaf |

Looking for the meaning of a word is one way of using a dictionary, but it can help you in other ways too. The next questions show you how.

C. Words which go together

Match a verb on the left with a noun on the right.
Use each word once only.

light	a car
paint	a cigarette
park	a letter
write	a picture

Some words often occur with other words; they form word partnerships. A good dictionary helps you to see which words often go together.

D. Word formation

Use the correct form of the word in parentheses to complete the sentence.

I'm Australian. What . . . . are you? (NATION)

Nobody's at work today. It's a . . . . holiday. (NATION)

What is the . . . . between a wine glass and a glass of wine? (DIFFER)

Can we go home a . . . . way? (DIFFER)

> Words often have different grammatical forms. A good dictionary will show you these.

E. The past tense

Complete the sentence by using the past tense of the verb in parentheses.

Yesterday morning she . . . . to school early. (COME)

She . . . . to the movies yesterday. (GO)

I . . . . $100 for that last year. (PAY)

We . . . . her last month. (SEE)

He . . . . teaching in 1987. (STOP)

> You need to know when a word is irregular; again your dictionary should help.

F. Pronunciation

Which of these words has a different vowel sound?

beer	clear	dear	near	wear
group	**south**	**soup**	**soon**	**route**

> When you learn a word you should make sure you know how to say it. This is why a good dictionary shows you the pronunciation of each word.

2 Verb square – 1

Complete the square by finding the verb missing from each sentence. The first letter of each word is the same as the last letter of the word before.

You can see the first verb as an example.

1. Let's . . . . ! Let's do the first one!
2. Can you . . . . me the way to the station?
3. Will the teacher . . . . you come in if you're late?
4. I'd like to . . . . you for all your help.
5. Please . . . . on the door before you go in.
6. You can . . . . the book. I don't need it.
7. Could you . . . . the groceries on the table?
8. Do you want me to . . . . your book back to the library?
9. What time does the movie . . . . ?
10. I don't have a lot of homework to . . . . tonight.
11. Would you like to . . . . your meal now?
12. It's very difficult to . . . . your writing.
13. I . . . . about her every night.
14. Can you . . . . me outside the town hall?
15. I have to . . . . to my father about it.
16. Mommy! Can you come and . . . . me goodnight?

1		2		3	4			5
S	**T**	**A**	**R**	**T**				

Use each of these verbs once only.

do	order
dream	put
end	read
keep	start
kiss	take
knock	talk
let	tell
meet	thank

16   6
15   7
14   8
13   12   11   10   9

3 Time expressions

Look at the following information:

JUNE						JULY						
S		4	11	18	25	S		2	9	16	23	30
M		5	12	19	26	M		3	10	17	24	31
Tu		6	13	20	27	Tu		4	11	18	25	
W		7	14	(21)	28	W		5	12	19	26	
Th	1	8	15	22	29	Th		6	13	20	27	
F	2	9	16	23	30	F		7	14	21	28	
S	3	10	17	24		S	1	8	15	22	29	

Today is Wednesday 21st June.

Put these expressions in the correct place.

the day after tomorrow	**next Tuesday**
the day before yesterday	**next weekend**
a couple of weeks ago	**today**
3 weeks time from now	**tomorrow**
last Friday	**a week from tomorrow**
last month	**yesterday afternoon**
last weekend	**yesterday morning**

1. May . . . .
2. June 7th . . . .
3. June 16th . . . .
4. June 17th,18th . . . .
5. June 19th . . . .
6. June 20th a.m. . . . .
7. June 20th p.m. . . . .
8. June 21st . . . . *today* . . . .
9. June 22nd . . . .
10. June 23rd . . . .
11. June 24th, 25th . . . .
12. June 27th . . . .
13. June 29th . . . .
14. July 12th . . . .

4 Plurals

Most nouns form their plurals by adding an 's', for example:

     student   students

Some nouns do not form their plural in this way.

This means that when you learn a new noun, you should always check how it forms its plural.

A.   Form the plural of each of the following nouns.

a. address . . . .   **g.** story   . . . .

b. box   . . . .   **h.** man   . . . .

c. boy   . . . .   **i.** potato . . . .

d. child . . . .   **j.** tomato . . . .

e. knife   . . . .   **k.** watch . . . .

f. leaf   . . . .   **l.** woman . . . .

B.   Complete each of the following sentences by using the plural form of one of the following nouns. Use each noun once only.

country	**day**	**foot**	**shelf**
beach	**dress**	**sandwich**	**tooth**

1. He always has two . . . . and an apple for lunch.

2. I brush my . . . . after every meal.

3. How many . . . . are your parents staying here?

4. California's . . . . are nicer than New Jersey's.

5. We have students from seventeen different . . . .

6. I need some more . . . . to put all my books on.

7. My . . . . hurt after all that running.

8. She wants to buy two new . . . . to wear on vacation.

5 Memory game

Can you name all the things in the picture? Use each of these words once:

razor	mushroom	scissors	bird	fork
gloves	hairbrush	glasses	arrow	puddle
parachute	spoon	bottle	envelope	robot
ring	tree	boat	pear	umbrella

Later in the book, you will be asked how many of these words you can remember — **without** looking at the words again!

6 Numbers

Complete each word to give the correct number.

Use one of the following words.

Use each word once only.

eight   five   seventy twelve
eleven   hundred ten   twenty
fifteen   seven   three

1. A soccer team has . . . . players.

2. Two feet have . . . . toes.

3. $50 - 30 =$

4. A week has . . . . days.

5. $9 + 6 =$

6. A century has a . . . . years.

7. A triangle has . . . . sides.

8. $25 \div 5 =$

9. A year has . . . . months.

10. $14 \times 5 =$

11. 2 hands = 2 thumbs + ... fingers.

What numbers are these? Fill in the missing letters.

12. _ E _ E _ _ _ - _ E _ E _ .

13. _ _ I _ _ Y - _ _ _ E E .

14. _ I _ _ _ - _ I _ .

15. _ I _ _ _ - _ I _ E .

12

7 Parts of the body

Use these words to label the dragon.

eye	toe	finger	shoulder
ear	elbow	hand	leg
tongue	mouth	arm	stomach
foot	neck	chest	heel

16. _____

15. _____

14. _____

13. _____

12. _____

11. _____

10. _____

9. _____

8. _____

1. _____

2. _____

3. _____

4. _____

5. _____

6. _____

7. _____

8 Jobs – word formation

Form the word for the person doing the job by putting an ending to the word in parentheses, for example:

Bill is a *teacher* . . . . at my school. (TEACH)

1. That . . . . paints beautiful pictures. (ART)

2. Your . . . . makes wonderful bread. (BAKE)

3. You pay the . . . . She's that lady over there. (CASH)

4. You can ask a . . . . about which medicine you need. (PHARMACY)

5. He's a famous ballet . . . . (DANCE)

6. On most buses you pay the . . . . (DRIVE)

7. He's a . . . . in a pop group. (DRUM)

8. Phone the . . . . if the lights don't work. (ELECTRIC)

9. If something goes wrong with the machine, tell the . . . . (ENGINE)

10. We have a . . . . who comes twice a week. (GARDEN)

11. My cousin is a . . . . for the Daily News. (WRITE)

12. Ask the . . . . if you can borrow this book. (LIBRARY)

13. He's the . . . . of a clothing store in town. (MANAGE)

14. That . . . . plays a lot of different instruments. (MUSIC)

15. Ask the . . . . to get the number for you. (OPERATE)

16. Do you know a good . . . . to paint my house? (PAINT)

17. The . . . . only had a small camera, but three HUGE lenses! (PHOTOGRAPH)

18. That . . . . plays very well. (PIANO)

19. I'm a . . . . on that ship. (SAIL)

20. I'm going to write a letter to the . . . . of this paper. (EDIT)

9 Sentence starters – 1

Here are three common ways of starting sentences. Can you complete them in each situation? There is a list of phrases at the bottom of the page to help you.

Could I....?

1.	You are in a restaurant. You want the menu.	Could I ....
2.	You are in a restaurant. You like fish.	Could I ....
3.	You need a pen. Your friend has two.	Could I ....
4.	The room is hot. The windows are shut.	Could I ....
5.	You're buying a new jacket. Is it the right size?	Could I ....

Could you....?

6.	You are on the phone. You can't hear the other person.	Could you ....
7.	Your friend is playing VERY loud music.	Could you ....
8.	You can't do this exercise. Your friend is very clever.	Could you ....
9.	You have missed the last bus. Your friend has a car.	Could you ....
10.	You can't find the post office. Ask someone.	Could you ....

I'd like....?

11.	You go into a hotel looking for a room for yourself.	I'd like ....
12.	You go into a restaurant with two friends.	I'd like ....
13.	You go into a bank to buy 10,000 pesetas.	I'd like ....
14.	You want to play tennis tomorrow. You call and say...	I'd like ....
15.	You want to fly to Paris as early as possible tomorrow.	I'd like ....

Useful phrases: turn it down, borrow a pen, change some money, have the fish, help me, try it on, a table for three, give me a lift, have the menu, reserve a court, an early flight to Paris, speak up, open a window, tell me the way, a single room.

10 Word groups – 1

It is helpful to make a list of the words you use when you talk about a subject. When you learn a new word, you can add it to one of your lists. This book will give you some ideas but why don't you think of some subjects you are interested in and see how many words you can put in a list?

Put each of the words below into the correct list.
Use each word once only.
Can you think of any more words to add to each list?

fall	green	purple	sun
brown	May	Saturday	Sunday
December	nineteen	seventy	twelve
eight	October	spring	Wednesday
February	orange	snow	wind
Friday	rain	summer	winter

1. COLORS

. . . .

. . . .

. . . .

. . . .

2. DAYS

. . . .

. . . .

. . . .

. . . .

3. MONTHS

. . . .

. . . .

. . . .

. . . .

4. NUMBERS

. . . .

. . . .

. . . .

. . . .

5. SEASONS

. . . .

. . . .

. . . .

. . . .

6. THE WEATHER

. . . .

. . . .

. . . .

. . . .

11 Word wheel – 1

Fill the wheel, using the clues. Each five-letter word starts at the edge of the wheel and ends in the center.
As you can see, they all end in the same letter.

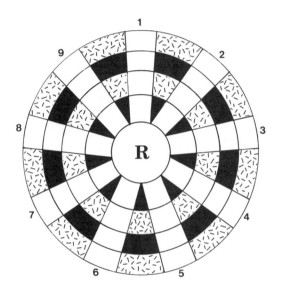

1. Not the winner.

2. A person who makes bread and cakes.

3. Can you put these in the right . . . .: 4213?

4. Be careful! The . . . . is wet. Watch out you don't slip!

5. You sit on one of these.

6. These instructions are not very . . . . I can't understand them at all.

7. The main . . . . which flows through Louisiana is the Mississippi.

8. Do you want cream and . . . . with your coffee?

9. Opposite of *always*.

12 Family tree

Look at the family tree and complete the sentences.
Use a word from the list on the right.

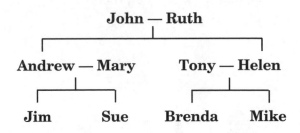

1.	John is Ruth's	**aunt**
2.	Ruth is Helen's	**cousin**
3.	Ruth is Tony's	**daughter**
4.	John is Helen's	**daughter-in-law**
5.	John is Tony's	**father**
6.	Helen is Ruth's	**father-in-law**
7.	Andrew is Ruth's	**granddaughter**
8.	Mary is John's	**grandfather**
9.	Tony is John's	**grandmother**
10.	John is Jim's	**grandson**
11.	Ruth is Sue's	**husband**
12.	Sue is John's	**mother**
13.	Jim is John's	**mother-in-law**
14.	Sue is Helen's	**nephew**
15.	Jim is Tony's	**niece**
16.	Andrew is Brenda's	**son**
17.	Mary is Brenda's	**son-in-law**
18.	Brenda is Sue's	**uncle**

13 Fruit and vegetables

Use these endings to complete the words below. Use each ending once only. The first one has been done as an example.

lon	apple	cumber	ple
nut	ar	ery	room
ana	ato	mon	rot
ange	cot	fruit	tuce

1. ap *ple* . . . . 2. apri . . . . 3. pot . . . . 4. car . . . .

5. coco . . . . 6. or . . . . 7. le . . . . 8. cu . . . .

9. me . . . . 10. grape . . . . . 11. ban . . . . 12. let . . . .

13. pe . . . . 14. pine . . . . . . 15. cel . . . . 16. mush . . . . .

14 Desk and table

Don't forget to keep making lists of words you use when you talk about a subject. See if you can think of more words to add to the lists in this exercise.

Where do you usually find each of these?
Put them into the correct list.

bowl	envelope	pen	spoon
cup	fork	pencil	stamp
calendar	glass	plate	napkin
dictionary	pitcher	ruler	telephone
dish	notebook	saucer	typewriter

1. OFFICE DESK

. . . .

. . . .

. . . .

. . . .

. . . .

. . . .

. . . .

. . . .

. . . .

. . . .

2. DINING TABLE

. . . .

. . . .

. . . .

. . . .

. . . .

. . . .

. . . .

. . . .

. . . .

. . . .

Now complete each sentence with the best word from the lists.

1. You need a . . . . if you want to draw a straight line.

2. Could you pass me the . . . . of water, please?

3. Oh no! My . . . . is ringing again!

4. I use the . . . . if I'm not sure how to spell a word.

5. I'm afraid there isn't a . . . . to eat my soup with.

6. The catalog is too big to fit inside this . . . .

15 Verb square – 2

Complete the square by finding the verb missing from each sentence.
The first letter of each word is the same as the last letter of the word
before.

You can see the first verb as an example.

1. We have to . . . . or we'll be late.
2. I can't . . . . you! Don't speak so softly!
3. He's going to . . . . in the race tomorrow.
4. You . . . . a good dictionary when you do these exercises.
5. Why does she . . . . her car so fast?
6. I always . . . . some fruit at the end of my meal.
7. Can you . . . . the ball back to those boys?
8. They always . . . . the same clothes.
9. I . . . . a newspaper every morning.
10. He says they . . . . too much coffee.
11. I really don't . . . . the answer to your question.
12. She often has to . . . . if the bus is late.
13. They always . . . . by air when they go to Dallas.
14. He's very funny. He always makes me . . . .
15. Do not want me to . . . . you to open the window?
16. Which do you . . . . — tea or coffee?

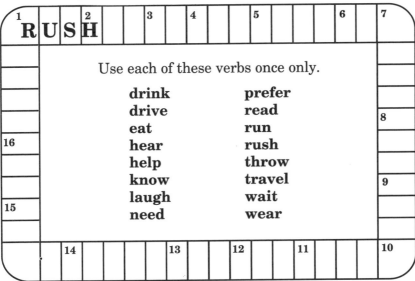

Use each of these verbs once only.

drink	prefer
drive	read
eat	run
hear	rush
help	throw
know	travel
laugh	wait
need	wear

16 Stress patterns

When you look up a word in the dictionary, you should make sure you know how to pronounce it. One problem is knowing where the stress is. Your dictionary should show you this.

In this exercise you must put each of the words below into the correct list depending on its stress pattern.
The sign ▼ shows the main stress.
The first word is shown as an example.

arrival	difficulty	mechanic	photograph
arrive	explain	music	photographer
belong	guitar	musician	garden
cabbage	librarian	origin	successful
calculator	luxurious	original	supermarket
centimeter	luxury	palace	sympathy

1. ▼○

. . . .

. . . .

. . . .

. . . .

2. ○▼

. . . .

. . . .

. . . .

. . . .

3. ▼○○

. . . .

. . . .

. . . .

. . . .

4. ○▼○

arrival . . . .

. . . .

. . . .

. . . .

5. ▼○○○

. . . .

. . . .

. . . .

. . . .

6. ○▼○○

. . . .

. . . .

. . . .

. . . .

17 Rooms of the house–1

You can help yourself to learn and remember more easily if you use what you have around you to learn English.
Sit in your room and ask yourself if you know the English word for each of the things you see. If not, find out.

Look at the picture of a bedroom. From the list below find the word for each item with a number on it. Use each word once only.

mirror	pillow	coat hanger	closet
comb	hot water bottle	lamp	pyjamas
alarm clock	hair dryer	bedspread	dresser
curtain	hair brush	lipstick	sheet

1. _____

2. _____

16. _____

15. _____

14. _____

13. _____

3. _____

4. _____

12. _____

11. _____

5. _____

6. _____

7. _____

10. _____

8. _____

9. _____

18 Around town

Choose the correct words to complete the sentences.
Look up any words you don't know.

1. There's a bus . . . . just outside my house.
   a. station   **b.** quay   **c.** stop   **d.** start

2. They're pulling down all those buildings to make room for a . . . . .
   a. parking   **b.** lane   **c.** mail box   **d.** parking lot

3. Where can I . . . . a bus to the movie theater?
   a. get in   **b.** catch   **c.** fetch   **d.** become

4. My train leaves from . . . . 7.
   a. quay   **b.** stop   **c.** track   **d.** park

5. She lives on the top floor of that apartment . . . .
   a. building   **b.** tower   **c.** construction **d.** block

6. We're going . . . . a guided tour of the town.
   a. on   **b.** at   **c.** in   **d.** by

7. I'll meet you outside the . . . . pool.
   a. swim   **b.** swimming   **c.** sport   **d.** football

8. You can see all the tourists slowly . . . . around the souvenir shops.
   a. marching   **b.** running   **c.** wandering   **d.** rushing

9. Don't walk in the street, children! Stay on the . . . . !
   a. way   **b.** sidewalk   **c.** route   **d.** street

10. I'm just going to . . . . a picture of the town square.
    a. take   **b.** make   **c.** do   **d.** have

11. This is a . . . . zone. No vehicles are allowed.
    a. traffic   **b.** pedestrian **c.** car   **d.** truck

12. I'll wait for you . . . . the corner of the street.
    a. in   **b.** inside   **c.** at   **d.** to

19 Opposites – 1

It is much easier to understand and remember the meaning of a word if you put it in a sentence, especially if you choose an interesting or amusing one.

When you add a word to your list of vocabulary, don't just put the definition with it but an example of how to use it.

Complete each sentence with the opposite of the word in parentheses. Choose from one of the following words. Use each word once only.

clean	light	open	small
cold	low	poor	tall
easy	loud	right	thin
good	old	slow	wet

1. He's very . . . . at his job. (BAD)

2. They live in a . . . . house in the country. (BIG)

3. She had . . . . brown hair. (DARK)

4. It's . . . . to get a job in this town. (DIFFICULT)

5. The room was very . . . . (DIRTY)

6. Clean it with a . . . . cloth. (DRY)

7. The traffic is very . . . . at 5.30. (FAST)

8. There was a . . . . wall around the house. (HIGH)

9. Could I have some more . . . . water, please? (HOT)

10. I'm going to wear my . . . . clothes. (NEW)

11. He always speaks in a very . . . . voice. (QUIET)

12. She comes from a very . . . . family. (RICH)

13. He's really . . . . and has white hair. (SHORT)

14. The door is still . . . . (CLOSED)

15. The ice was very . . . . in some places. (THICK)

16. That's the . . . . answer to the question. (WRONG)

20 Which job is it?

Choose the best word to complete the sentence.
Look up any words you don't know.

1. Ask the store . . . . where the detergent is.
   a. nurse   **b.** assistant   **c.** barber   **d.** conductor

2. That . . . . sells very good meat.
   a. baker   **b.** dentist   **c.** architect   **d.** butcher

3. If my tooth doesn't stop hurting, I'll go and see my . . . .
   a. actor   **b.** dentist   **c.** writer   **d.** jockey

4. Not many buses have a . . . . You usually pay the driver.
   a. manager   **b.** farmer   **c.** conductor   **d.** porter

5. Look! The . . . . is feeding the lions.
   a. keeper   **b.** pianist   **c.** postman   **d.** engineer

6. The . . . . is showing them his plans of the new building.
   a. optician   **b.** nurse   **c.** architect   **d.** dancer

7. She wants the . . . . to make a special cake for her daughter's birthday.
   a. inspector   **b.** baker   **c.** cashier   **d.** mechanic

8. My . . . . always comes early so I get my letters before I go to work.
   a. mailman   **b.** pharmacist   **c.** butcher   **d.** porter

9. The boss wants her . . . . to take some dictation.
   a. secretary   **b.** novelist   **c.** conductor   **d.** journalist

10. The . . . . gives the patient his medicine twice a day.
    a. butcher   **b.** nurse   **c.** operator   **d.** pianist

11. I hope the . . . . can repair our car quickly.
    a. mechanic   **b.** reporter   **c.** surgeon   **d.** coach

12. After your eye test, the . . . . will tell you if you need glasses or not.
    a. engineer   **b.** mechanic   **c.** clown   **d.** optician

13. The . . . . wanted to write an article about me in the paper.
    a. agent   **b.** musician   **c.** journalist   **d.** hairdresser

14. The . . . . will take your suitcases to your room.
    a. porter   **b.** author   **c.** engineer   **d.** jockey

21 Expressions with 'that's'

Match the responses on the right to the remarks on the left to make eight conversations.

1. Sorry I'm late.

a. That's funny.

2. Can I pay you later?

b. That's fine by me.

3. I'm sure I left my coat here, but I can't see it anywhere.

c. That's all right.

4. You did say $90, didn't you?

d. Yes, that's right.

5. He definitely took your $10 bill. Should I call the police?

e. That's not quite what I meant.

6. It was crazy but he is very young.

f. That's beside the point.

7. So how much do you earn?

g. That's taking things a bit too far.

8. You don't like Americans? So you don't like me, then?

h. That's none of your business.

1		2		3		4		5		6		7		8	

Remember using fixed expressions like these makes your English more natural.

22 Nouns for people – 1

When you look up a word in a dictionary, notice what other words can be formed from it, for example:

act   **action**   **active**   **activity**   **actor**

Sometimes you find these extra words with the definition of the original word and sometimes they have their own definition. This means it is a good idea to check the words before and after every new word you look up.

Form the word for the person by putting an ending to the word given, for example:

She's a very good *worker* . . . . (WORK)

1. That . . . . speaks too quickly. (ANNOUNCE)
2. He's a good . . . . He wins all his fights. (BOX)
3. The police are looking for a dangerous . . . . (CRIME)
4. The . . . . wants to interview all of us. (DETECT)
5. I try to speak clearly when I meet a . . . . (FOREIGN)
6. Our . . . . makes us practice a lot. (INSTRUCT)
7. She's the . . . . of this machine. (INVENT)
8. Who is the . . . . of that group? (LEAD)
9. Can I have a . . . . at my party? (MAGIC)
10. Do you know the . . . . of this book? (WRITE)
11. Are you the . . . . of this car? (OWN)
12. He talks so much because he's a . . . . (POLITICS)
13. The . . . . wants to know everything about me. (REPORT)
14. That . . . . is going very fast! (RIDE)
15. Do you think that man with a gun is a . . . .? (ROB)
16. If you're a . . . . , you have to work hard. (SCIENCE)
17. She's a . . . . at the same college as me. (STUDY)
18. She's a . . . . so you must be polite. (VISIT)

23 Where was it said?

In which of the buildings on the right were the following said?

1. What kind of property did you have in mind?
2. Two for the 8:30 show, please.
3. And an air-mail sticker, please.
4. I can't sell them to you without a prescription.
5. Could you check the oil, please?
6. I've got a reservation in the name of Jones.
7. A large sliced loaf, please.
8. Just a trim, please.
9. Have you thought about bifocals?
10. I'm just going to listen to your chest.
11. You will pay a fine of $300.
12. Smile, please. Say cheese!
13. Would you prefer a digital one?
14. How much for a round trip to New York from San Francisco?

a. MOVIE THEATER	b. PHARMACY
c. DOCTOR'S	d. REAL ESTATE AGENCY
e. BAKERY	f. HAIR-DRESSER'S
g. AUTO SHOP	h. JEWELER'S
i. COURT	j. PHOTO-STUDIO
k. POST OFFICE	l. OPTICIAN'S
m. HOTEL	n. TRAVEL AGENCY

Write your answers here.

1	2	3	4	5	6	7	8	9	10	11	12	13	14

Can you think of anything else that might be said in these buildings?

24 Signs

If you go to an English-speaking country or see one in a movie, look at the signs. You can often get useful vocabulary from them.
Make lists of places where you see signs and write examples of the kind of signs you might find there.

Match the signs below with the places where they might be seen.
Where do you think you might see the other sign?
Can you think of any more signs you might see?

Choose from these places:

a bank	a phone booth
a bookstore	a mail box
a park	a gas station
a children's playground	a supermarket
a football field	a theater
a hotel restaurant	a train
outside a hotel bedroom	a zoo

NO CAMPING	DO NOT DISTURB	SCIENCE FICTION

1. . . . .   2. . . . .   3. . . . .

PLEASE RETURN ALL SHOPPING CARTS	TODAY'S EXCHANGE RATES	KICK-OFF 3 P.M.

4. . . . .   5. . . . .   6. . . . .

| SELF-SERVE | INTERNATIONAL FLIGHTS ONLY | FOR EMERGENCY CALLS DIAL 911 |

7. . . . .   8. . . . .   9. . . . .

| DO NOT LEAN OUT OF THE WINDOWS | OPEN TO NON-RESIDENTS | EVENING PERFORMANCE 7.30 |

10. . . . .   11. . . . .   12. . . . .

| LAST PICK-UP 5:30 | NO DOGS, NO BALL GAMES | PLEASE DO NOT FEED THE ANIMALS |

13. . . . .   14. . . . .   15. . . . .

25 Expressions with 'make'

Complete each sentence with one of these words to make a fixed expression with the verb *make*.

tracks	deal	difference	most	wish	amends	big		tails
sick	ends	clear		while	sure	it	big deal	sense

1. I would like to make it . . . . before we start, there will be no talking during the ceremony.

2. Before we leave let me make . . . . I've turned off all the lights.

3. Don't forget to make a . . . . before you blow out the candles, dear.

4. I know you have your reservations about joining our company but I assure you that if you do we could make it worth your . . . .

5. I'd like to stay, but I really ought to make . . . .

6. I hope to be making more money next year but right now the business is just managing to make . . . . meet.

7. We were stuck in that elevator for three hours but we decided to make the . . . . out of the unfortunate situation and tell jokes.

8. She's so rich she makes me . . . .

9. I've been reading and re-reading this instruction manual for over an hour now but I still can't seem to make heads or . . . . of it.

10. It's not easy to make it . . . . in show business.

11. I'll make you a . . . . – you give me a ride home and I'll make you dinner. Sound good?

12. I finished my work in time to come to the party but Karen was really busy and couldn't make . . . .

13. Yes I did win first prize in the West Coast Swing dance contest but you don't have to make such a . . . . about it.

14. It really doesn't make much . . . . whether you finish today or do it tomorrow.

15. I listened to all the reasons he had for dropping out of college but it still doesn't make any . . . . to me.

16. I realize that I ruined your party, so I've come to make . . . . if it isn't too late.

Now underline all the expressions which contain *make*.

26 What's missing? – 1

Under each picture write the name of the item and what is missing.
Choose from the following list of words.
The first has been done for you.

airplane	handle	page
arm	house	roof
armchair	pitcher	table
book	leg	teapot
button	lid	wheel
car	jacket	wing

1. *book*
    page

2. . . . .
    . . . .

3. . . . .
    . . . .

4. . . . .
    . . . .

5. . . . .
    . . . .

6. . . . .
    . . . .

7. . . . .
    . . . .

8. . . . .
    . . . .

9. . . . .
    . . . .

27 Word formation – 1

Remember that when you look up a word in a dictionary, you should see if any other words can be formed from it. Grouping these words together should help you remember them, for example:

direct direction directly director directory

Change the word in parentheses to complete the sentence.

1. We are waiting for the . . . . of his plane. (ARRIVE)

2. There was a . . . . to find the best cook. (COMPETE)

3. We must make a . . . . about where to go. (DECIDE)

4. The train made a late . . . . (DEPART)

5. The boss wants you to take some . . . . (DICTATE)

6. What kind of . . . . is there in this town? (ENTERTAIN)

7. There's some new . . . . in the laboratory. (EQUIP)

8. Could you repeat that . . . . ? (EXPLAIN)

9. He had a strange . . . . on his face. (EXPRESS)

10. Put the ice-cream in the . . . . , please. (FREEZE)

11. Is there any more . . . . about the accident? (INFORM)

12. You must read the . . . . to this book. (INTRODUCE)

13. I have an . . . . to a party tonight. (INVITE)

14. Are you going to the . . . . tomorrow? (MEET)

15. That . . . . is by Picasso. (PAINT)

16. . . . . is my favorite hobby. (PHOTOGRAPH)

17. What's the correct . . . . of this word? (PRONOUNCE)

18. I have a lot of . . . . to do. (SHOP)

28 Word ladder

Change the top word into the word at the bottom. Use the clues to help you. Each time you change one letter only in the previous word. Sometimes you might not know the word but you can guess what is possible and check with your dictionary.
Remember, guessing and using a good dictionary are two important ways to help you to improve your English.

	RISE
2. Fruit ready to be eaten.	
3. Thick string.	
4. One of the parts in a play, taken by an actor.	
5. Either of the two ends of the earth's axis.	
6. White in the face.	
7. Put one thing on top of another.	
8. A folder for keeping papers together.	
9. 1,609 meters.	
10. Would you like a . . . . shake?	
11. Where flour is made.	
12. Your glass is empty. Can I . . . . it up for you?	
13. . . . . you come and see me tomorrow?	
14. He built an enormous . . . . around his house.	
15. Go on foot.	
16. Speak.	
17. Not short.	
	FALL

29 Word partnerships – 1

Some pairs of words often occur together. If you see one of them, you can expect to see the other. This makes listening and reading easier! Here are some partnerships.

Match the verb on the left with a noun on the right. Use each word once only. Write your answers in the boxes.

Set 1

1.	ask	**a.**	a bicycle		1	
2.	climb	**b.**	a boat		2	
3.	drink	**c.**	a car		3	
4.	drive	**d.**	a cigarette		4	
5.	eat	**e.**	a cup of coffee		5	
6.	fly	**f.**	a mountain		6	
7.	light	**g.**	a plane		7	
8.	ride	**h.**	a question		8	
9.	sail	**i.**	a sandwich		9	
10.	tell	**j.**	a story		10	

Set 2

Now do the same with these words.

1.	build	**a.**	a drink		1	
2.	comb	**b.**	a game		2	
3.	cook	**c.**	your hair		3	
4.	pack	**d.**	a house		4	
5.	play	**e.**	a letter		5	
6.	pour	**f.**	a light		6	
7.	sing	**g.**	a meal		7	
8.	stick on	**h.**	a song		8	
9.	turn on	**i.**	a stamp		9	
10.	write	**j.**	a suitcase		10	

30 Clothes –1

Think about the clothes you wear. Look at pictures of clothes in newspapers and magazines. Do you know what to call them in English? If not, find out.
Why don't you make your own picture dictionary? Cut out pictures of clothes, stick them in a book and put their names in English next to them. This will help you to remember things better.

Can you name twelve things Fido is wearing? Use each of these once:

shoelace	sweater	apron	shorts
bow tie	bra	T-shirt	scarf
cap	sneaker	sandal	vest

1. _____

12. _____

11. _____

2. _____

3. _____

4. _____

10. _____

5. _____

6. _____

9. _____

7. _____

8. _____

31 Word groups – 2

Are you making lists of words you use when talking about a subject?
Remember to think not only of nouns but also of verbs and adjectives you
can use. The same words often occur together.
Learning them together can make them easier to remember.

Put each of the words below into the correct list.
Use each word once only.
Can you think of any more words to add to each list?

bird watching	cow	knitting	stamp collecting
brake	credit card	lion	steer
cash	exercise book	photography	teach
cat	feed	pupil	traveler's check
check book	headlight	rectangular	triangular
circular	homework	square	tire

1. ANIMALS

. . . .

. . . .

. . . .

. . . .

2. THE CAR

. . . .

. . . .

. . . .

. . . .

3. HOBBIES

. . . .

. . . .

. . . .

. . . .

4. MONEY

. . . .

. . . .

. . . .

. . . .

5. SCHOOL

. . . .

. . . .

. . . .

. . . .

6. SHAPES

. . . .

. . . .

. . . .

. . . .

32 Where do they work?

Match each person with the place where she/he works.
Use each item once only.

1.	artist	a.	bakery
2.	astronomer	b.	circus
3.	baker	c.	embassy
4.	clown	d.	hotel
5.	hairdresser	e.	flower shop
6.	diplomat	f.	ambulance
7.	florist	g.	autoshop
8.	jockey	h.	library
9.	keeper	i.	observatory
10.	librarian	j.	racetrack
11.	mechanic	k.	restaurant
12.	professor	l.	school
13.	paramedic	m.	studio
14.	teacher	n.	salon
15.	bellboy	o.	university
16.	waiter/waitress	p.	zoo

Write your answers here:

1	2	3	4	5	6	7	8	9	10	11	12	13	14	15	16

Can you think of any other people who work in these places?

33 Opposites – 2

Complete each sentence with the opposite of the word given.
Choose from one of the following words. Use each word once only.

absent	early	happy	noisy
asleep	empty	hard	short
dangerous	expensive	interesting	strong
dark	fat	light	young

1. He was still . . . . when she came home. (AWAKE)

2. This is a very . . . . movie. (BORING)

3. The watches in this store are very . . . . (CHEAP)

4. All her children have . . . . hair. (FAIR)

5. I noticed that his glass was . . . . again. (FULL)

6. He was surprised that the suitcase was so . . . . (HEAVY)

7. I think I'll catch the . . . . bus tomorrow. (LATE)

8. The commute to work is really . . . . (LONG)

9. She thinks her daughter's boyfriend is too . . . . for her. (OLD)

10. Is Carlos . . . . today? (PRESENT)

11. Our neighbors are very . . . . (QUIET)

12. The news made her very . . . . (SAD)

13. It's . . . . to swim there. (SAFE)

14. The butter was too . . . . to use. (SOFT)

15. His wife was worried because he was so . . . . (THIN)

16. I don't like this coffee. It's much too . . . . (WEAK)

34 Word partnerships – 2

Remember to note down pairs of words which often occur together. These word partnerships will help you understand spoken and written English. Hearing **one** word, helps you to **expect** the other, so it is easier to understand.

Match the adjective on the left with a noun on the right. Use each word once only. Write your answers in the boxes.

Set 1

1.	alphabetical	**a.**	bed	1	
2.	chocolate	**b.**	bar	2	
3.	cloudy	**c.**	coffee	3	
4.	digital	**d.**	hair	4	
5.	double	**e.**	knife	5	
6.	instant	**f.**	laugh	6	
7.	loud	**g.**	order	7	
8.	sharp	**h.**	road	8	
9.	wavy	**i.**	sky	9	
10.	wide	**j.**	watch	10	

Set 2

Now do the same with these words.

1.	bald	**a.**	banana	1	
2.	classical	**b.**	beef	2	
3.	curly	**c.**	clothes	3	
4.	direct	**d.**	couple	4	
5.	fashionable	**e.**	door	5	
6.	front	**f.**	drink	6	
7.	married	**g.**	flight	7	
8.	non-alcoholic	**h.**	hair	8	
9.	ripe	**i.**	head	9	
10.	roast	**j.**	music	10	

35 Past tense – 1

Most verbs form their past by adding 'd' or 'ed', for example:

arrive   arrived   start   started

Some verbs do not form their past tense so easily. There are about 200 irregular verbs in English. About 100 of these are common so you should always check the past tense of any new verb you learn.

Find the past form of the following verbs:

blow   break   cut   find   get   give   grow   hear
keep   make   put   run   send   take   think   throw

The words can go across or down, or diagonally left to right. The same letter may be used in more than one word. The past form of 'blow' is shown as an example.

```
W I S E N T H R E W
G R I P O H E V E R
R A N U T O E L T O
E E L T C U B E M N
W B R A K G A V E G
T Y P E X H O L D M
T O E C U T I T T A
B R O K E H E A R D
C A S K F O U N D E
C A R K E P T A D Y
```

Many of the common verbs in English combine with an adverb or a preposition to form two-word verbs. For example, if you **look up** a word in your dictionary it means that you find information about it.

Look up some common English verbs and see how many examples of these kinds of combinations you can find.

A. Complete each of the sentences by using the past form of one of the verbs on the left and combining it with one of the words on the right. Use each verb once only. The first is shown as an example.

break	**find**	**get**	**grow**	**down**	**from**	**off**
hear	**keep**	**make**	**take**	**on**	**out**	**up**

1. We never .. *found out* ...... why he lost his job.

2. I'm sure he .... that story. It can't be true!

3. She .... in London and left when she was 16.

4. The car .... at the intersection and I couldn't start it again.

5. I .... late so I had no time for breakfast.

6. The interruption didn't stop him. He .... speaking.

7. The plane .... at 9 o'clock, 3 hours late.

8. I finally .... Henry last week. He phoned me from work.

B. Now do the same thing with these verbs and the words on the right.

blow	**cut**	**give**	**put**	**away**	**for**	**into**
run	**send**	**think**	**throw**	**off**	**over**	**up**

1. She .... the clothes she didn't need any more.

2. The bus stopped suddenly and the car .... the back of it.

3. He .... smoking when his doctor told him how dangerous it was.

4. It was raining so heavily that they .... the game until the following week.

5. They .... the doctor and he came immediately.

6. It was an offer he .... very carefully before he made his decision.

7. They .... the bridge with dynamite.

8. The telephone operator accidentally .... our conversation when she pressed the wrong button.

36 Nouns for people – 2

Form the word for the person by putting an ending to the word given, for example:

He's a *stranger* in this town. (STRANGE)

1. An . . . . should be good at math. (ACCOUNT)

2. Every . . . . hopes to discover a new star. (ASTRONOMY)

3. The . . . . sat there asking for money. (BEG)

4. He's a well-known . . . . on the radio. (BROADCAST)

5. Look out! That crazy . . . . is going too fast! (CYCLE)

6. Alfred Hitchcock was a famous movie . . . . (DIRECT)

7. Every . . . . dreams of winning a fortune. (GAMBLE)

8. She was the . . . . of last month's competition. (WIN)

9. She was the only . . . . left in the town. (INHABIT)

10. Her . . . . wants $10,000 for her safe return. (KIDNAP)

11. Their . . . . thinks they might go to prison. (LAW)

12. Since she's the oldest, she'll be the . . . . (LEAD)

13. His ambition is to be a . . . . one day. (MILLION)

14. Agatha Christie is a . . . . famous for her detective stories. (NOVEL)

15. The hotel . . . . asked them to register. (RECEPTION)

16. They've caught a drug . . . . at the airport. (SMUGGLE)

17. You should see a . . . . about that leg. (SPECIAL)

18. The candidate sent a letter to every . . . . (VOTE)

37 Food two-word expressions

Join one word on the left with one from the right to make a two-word partnership. Some words in the right column may be used more than once. Write your answers in the boxes.

1.	box	a.	bag	1	
2.	candy	b.	bar	2	
3.	cocktail	c.	break	3	
4.	coffee	d.	breakfast	4	
5.	continental	e.	dinner	5	
6.	doggie	f.	food	6	
7.	finger	g.	hour	7	
8.	happy	h.	luck	8	
9.	junk	i.	lunch	9	
10.	left	j.	meal	10	
11.	pot	k.	order	11	
12.	salad	l.	overs	12	
13.	side	m.	party	13	
14.	square	n.	stop	14	
15.	truck			15	
16.	TV			16	

Now complete each sentence with one of the compound nouns.

1. I couldn't finish that huge meal. I'm going to ask the waiter for a . . . .

2. We had a . . . . on Saturday. Everyone brought something delicious.

3. If we get to the bar in time for . . . . we'll get two drinks for the price of one.

4. After the ball game I didn't feel like cooking so I pulled a . . . . out of the freezer and heated it in the microwave.

38 Word formation – 2

Change each word to complete the sentence, for example:

Be *careful* . . . . when you open the door. (CARE)

1. This is my favorite chair. It's so . . . . ! (COMFORT)

2. It's . . . . to drive so fast. (DANGER)

3. I must clean this . . . . floor. (DIRT)

4. Elvis Presley was a . . . . pop singer. (FAME)

5. It was . . . . so they had to drive very slowly. (FOG)

6. Is lunch ready yet? They're very . . . . (HUNGER)

7. Be careful. The roads are very . . . . (ICE)

8. I'd like a nice . . . . orange. (JUICE)

9. How many . . . . holidays do you have? (NATION)

10. Why do they give such . . . . parties? (NOISE)

11. His broken arm is still very . . . . (PAIN)

12. The President was a very . . . . man. (POWER)

13. The children always get bored on a . . . . day. (RAIN)

14. He always feels . . . . in the morning. (SLEEP)

15. I live in the . . . . part of the country. (SOUTH)

16. The book was . . . . and he became very rich. (SUCCESS)

17. I hope we have . . . . weather for our vacation. (SUN)

18. We have a . . . . newspaper in this town. (WEEK)

19. Thanks for everything. I had a . . . . time. (WONDER)

20. He lives in a . . . . house by the sea. (WOOD)

39   Expressions with 'and'

Supply the second part of each fixed expression using one of the words given below. Use each word only once.

see   sound   simple   span   forget   order   square   clear   bones   well

1. You can't hold a grudge against him your whole life. Sometimes you just have to

   FORGIVE and . . . .

2. A lot of people complain that the last Super Bowl the Dallas Cowboys played in wasn't fair since they had home-field advantage, but they won

   FAIR and   . . . .

3. I know it takes a while to adjust to life in the college dormitories, but you'll get used to it, just

   WAIT and   . . . .

4. This place is a mess! Next Thursday is already Thanksgiving and before your parents come over for turkey we need to have this place looking

   SPICK and   . . . .

5. Whenever there's an earthquake in California, calls flood in from relatives in other places making sure that their loved ones are all

   SAFE and   . . . .

6. These days if you want to get a real good job you have to go to college

   PURE and   . . . .

7. Tom used to be pretty chunky, but since he started dieting and going to aerobics he's turned to

   SKIN and   . . . .

8. Before the landlord came and fixed this wall I could hear everything the neighbors were doing

   LOUD and   . . . .

9. I never found out whatever became of my old grammar school math teacher, but I'm sure she's still

   ALIVE and   . . . .

10. It seems to me that I always see police officers eating in donut shops when they really should be keeping

    LAW and   . . . .

40 Food and drink

Choose the best words to complete the sentences.

Look up any words you don't know.

1. I've got to have a drink. I'm so . . . .
   a. dirty **b.** hungry **c.** thirsty **d.** thirty

2. What vegetables would you like? . . . . , please.
   a. Peaches and carrots **b.** Peas and potatoes
   c. Tomatoes and pears **d.** Beans and apples

3. Is he going to . . . . the meal?
   a. pay **b.** bite **c.** feed **d.** pay for

4. Look in the oven and see if the . . . . is ready yet.
   a. cake **b.** ice cream **c.** soup **d.** boiled egg

5. This isn't very sweet. I'll add some more . . . .
   a. salt **b.** pepper **c.** vinegar **d.** sugar

6. I think I'll have . . . . for dessert.
   a. spaghetti **b.** apple pie **c.** a starter **d.** mustard

7. I need the frying pan so that I can make the . . . .
   a. salad **b.** toast **c.** honey **d.** omelette

8. I'd like my . . . . rare, please.
   a. tea **b.** chop **c.** steak **d.** chicken

9. Why is the waiter taking so long to . . . . us?
   a. save **b.** serve **c.** reserve **d.** order

10. I've got time for a very quick . . . . before I go.
    a. snack **b.** barbecue **c.** feast **d.** picnic

11. All he wants is two thin . . . . of roast beef.
    a. legs **b.** wings **c.** crusts **d.** slices

12. Have you got enough money to . . . . the bill?
    a. pay for **b.** pay **c.** buy **d.** spend

13. He's putting a lot of strawberry . . . . on his bread.
    a. marmalade **b.** pastry **c.** ham **d.** jam

14. I'm so . . . . , mom! Can I have something to eat?
    a. hungry **b.** angry **c.** thirsty **d.** sweet

15. I'll just . . . . the soup to see if it's all right.
    a. chew **b.** toast **c.** taste **d.** cut

16. A glass of . . . . , please. I never drink alcohol.
    a. orange juice **b.** whisky **c.** wine **d.** beer

41 Things used at work–1

Match each person with the thing she/he uses.

Use each item once only.

1. artist	**a.** camera		
2. baker	**b.** cash register		
3. cashier	**c.** drill		
4. housekeeper	**d.** ladder		
5. dentist	**e.** microphone	
6. farmer	**f.** oven	
7. hairdresser	**g.** paint brush	
8. librarian	**h.** rifle	
9. nurse	**i.** scissors	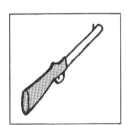
10. photographer	**j.** card index	
11. referee	**k.** thermometer	
12. singer	**l.** tractor	
13. soldier	**m.** tray	
14. secretary	**n.** computer	
15. waiter	**o.** vacuum cleaner	
16. window cleaner	**p.** whistle	

Write your answers here:

1	2	3	4	5	6	7	8	9	10	11	12	13	14	15	16

Can you think of any more things these people could use at work?

42 Which person is it?

Choose the best word to complete the sentence.

Look up any words you don't know.

1. Every . . . . in this army should know how to use the new gun.
   a. sailor   **b.** porter   **c.** soldier   **d.** joker

2. He left his job because his . . . . didn't pay him enough money.
   a. employee   **b.** employer   **c.** conductor   **d.** architect

3. The . . . . arrested him for stealing the diamonds.
   a. dentist   **b.** electrician   **c.** politician   **d.** policeman

4. A famous . . . . operated on her.
   a. surgeon   **b.** coach   **c.** driver   **d.** carpenter

5. The . . . . made a lot of noise as they left the party in their cars.
   a. thieves   **b.** characters   **c.** pedestrians   **d.** guests

6. It's difficult to be a . . . . of this club.
   a. travel agent   **b.** member   **c.** clown   **d.** bachelor

7. I can hear my next-door . . . . playing his trumpet.
   a. thief   **b.** customer   **c.** neighbor   **d.** champion

8. He hates marriage. He wants to stay a . . . .
   a. passenger   **b.** bachelor   **c.** customer   **d.** widow

9. Who is the . . . . of this book?
   a. author   **b.** surgeon   **c.** journalist   **d.** orphan

10. If she beats her, she'll be the new tennis . . . .
    a. character   **b.** host   **c.** champion   **d.** passenger

11. The . . . . made this door badly. I can't close it.
    a. orphan   **b.** carpenter   **c.** artist   **d.** pedestrian

12. After his parents died, the young . . . . went to live with his aunt.
    a. clown   **b.** farmer   **c.** orphan   **d.** lawyer

13. Sherlock Holmes is an important . . . . in detective fiction.
    a. employer   **b.** character   **c.** manager   **d.** writer

14. I hope they find the . . . . who stole my money.
    a. thief   **b.** orphan   **c.** champion   **d.** contestant

43 Word wheel – 2

Fill the wheel, using the clues. Each five-letter word starts at the edge of the wheel and ends in the center.
As you can see, they all end in the same letter.

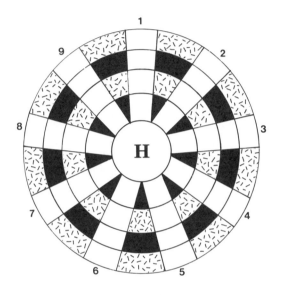

1. There's a bus coming. If we hurry, we'll . . . . it.
2. Go to the dentist if you have trouble with them.
3. The planet we live on.
4. Can you get a . . . . ? I've spilled water everywhere.
5. Do you have the time? I'm sure my . . . . is slow.
6. The end of life.
7. The opposite of *smooth*.
8. That's a bad . . . . ; you need some medicine for your throat.
9. Do you have a . . . . , please? I want to light my pipe.

There are lots of way of making **groups** of words — the same topic; words which often occur together; labels for parts of the same picture etc. It is always easier to learn and remember words if you study them in groups or as part of a picture or shape.

44 Conjunctions

Match the two halves of the sentences.
Use each half once only.

1.	He was very tired and it was very late	**a.**	unless the bus comes soon.
2.	They couldn't buy any ice-cream	**b.**	after I'd been living in New York for 12 years.
3.	He decided to go by plane	**c.**	so he didn't get a good grade.
4.	They spoke to the old man very slowly	**d.**	if you promise not to drive it too fast.
5.	Some of the questions on the test were very hard	**e.**	before her father came home.
6.	Take an umbrella with you	**f.**	while I was taking a bath.
7.	She told her boyfriend that he should leave	**g.**	until she found some she liked.
8.	Unfortunately the phone rang	**h.**	but he still didn't go to bed.
9.	You can borrow the car	**i.**	although he hated flying.
10.	She tried on at least 12 pairs of shoes	**j.**	so that he could understand what they were saying.
11.	I became an American citizen	**k.**	because they didn't have enough money.
12.	We'll be late for work	**l.**	in case it rains.

Write your answers here:

1	2	3	4	5	6	7	8	9	10	11	12

Did you notice how the conjunctions were used?
Make a list of the conjunctions here:

. . . .

. . . .

. . . .

Can you write your own sentences using each one? If you do this it will
help you to remember the words.

45 Conversations in town

Match the first part of the conversation on the left with the other part on the right.

1.	I'd like some roses, please.	a.	Do you want to send it airmail?
2.	Can you read the letters on the bottom line?	b.	Should I leave it long in the back?
3.	How long have you had the pain?	c.	Yes, but not two together, I'm afraid.
4.	I'd like a room for two nights, please.	d.	I'm not sure about the first one.
5.	I'd like to cash this check, please.	e.	How big a bunch would you like?
6.	Do you have anything in the back?	f.	Do you have any kind of identification?
7.	I'd like it short at the sides, please.	g.	Three times a day.
8.	A stamp for Brazil, please.	h.	Pork or beef?
9.	How often do you brush them?	i.	Single or double?
10.	A pound of sausages, please.	j.	Since last Friday.

Now match each conversation with a building below. One is done for you as an example; you must complete the others.
There will be one building left. Can you think of any conversations people might have there?

OPTICIAN'S	DOCTOR'S	LA BAMBA RESTAURANT	BANK	BUTCHER'S

CHAPLIN ROAD

PAVILION THEATER	BARBER'S	DENTIST'S	POST OFFICE	AVON HOTEL	FLORIST
					1 e

46 Pronunciation

Knowing how to pronounce a word is sometimes a problem. It may be difficult at first, but it is a very good idea to learn the symbols used for the different sounds in English. A good dictionary should have a list of the symbols it uses. You can then look up the pronunciation of any word you are not sure about.

Here are some exercises to give you practice in finding out how words are pronounced.

A. Pronunciation of 'ear'

'ear' can be pronounced

/ eə / as in 'bear'   /ɪə / as in 'dear'

Make words by putting one letter in front of 'ear' and then put your word in the correct pronunciation list.
Be careful! One word can be pronounced both ways.

/ eə /	/ɪə /	
bear	*dear*	
. . . .	. . . .	. . . .
. . . .	. . . .	. . . .
. . . .	. . . .	. . . .
. . . .	. . . .	. . . .

B. Pronunciation of 'ch'

'ch' can be pronounced

/ k / as in 'chemistry'   / tʃ / as in 'chair'

Put these words into the correct list depending on the way in which the 'ch' is pronounced.

ache	character	choose	handkerchief
bachelor	cheese	each	mechanic
branch	check	echo	scheme
change	chimney	exchange	school

/ k /	/ t∫ /	
chemistry	*chair*	. . . .
. . . .	. . . .	. . . .
. . . .	. . . .	. . . .
. . . .	. . . .	. . . .
. . . .	. . . .	. . . .
. . . .	. . . .	. . . .
. . . .	. . . .	. . . .

C.   Pronunciation of 'g'

'g' can be pronounced

/ g / as in 'girl'   / dʒ/ as in 'age'

Put these words into the correct list depending on the way in which the 'g' is pronounced.

again	**general**	**gift**	**margarine**
age	**generous**	**gymnastics**	**passenger**
begin	**get**	**magic**	**sugar**
girl	**giant**	**magazine**	**together**

/ g /	/ dʒ /
girl	*age*
. . . .	. . . .
. . . .	. . . .
. . . .	. . . .
. . . .	. . . .
. . . .	. . . .
. . . .	. . . .
. . . .	. . . .
. . . .	. . . .

> Remember, you don't really 'know' a new word until you know what it means **and** how to pronounce it!

47 Past tense – 2

Remember to check if a verb is irregular when you learn a new one.
Remember also that some verbs that end in **—ed** in their past form have
changes in their spelling, for example:

try   tried   stop   stopped

A good dictionary should show you these spelling changes.

Find the past form of the following verbs:

bring	carry	catch	come	do	fall	go	hang
hold	leave	read	see	sell	set	stand	wear

The words can go across or down, or diagonally left to right. The same
letter may be used in more than one word.
The past form of 'see' is shown as an example.

```
B  R  O  U  T  H  U  N  G  T
C  L  A  W  R  E  A  D  H  A
A  S  F  E  L  L  T  G  O  R
U  O  I  N  O  D  U  U  C  W
G  L  S  T  O  O  D  S  A  I
H  D  W  O  R  E  A  S  M  N
T  R  I  B  E  D  I  D  E  T
B  R  O  U  G  H  T  U  F  T
G  O  O  D  D  A  L  E  F  T
B  Y  E  C  A  R  R  I  E  D
```

Are you making lists of combinations of verbs with an adverb or a
preposition? Remember these are very common in English. Here are some
more examples. When you look them up, notice what other combinations
you can make with the verbs.

You need to learn the combination in the same way you learn new words.
Often you can guess the meaning of the combination from the meaning of
the basic word.

A. Complete each of the sentences by using the past form of one of the verbs on the left and combining it with one of the words on the right. Use each verb once only. The first is shown as an example.

bring	carry	come	do		across	on	out
go	leave	read	stand		through	up	without

1. The lights . . . . *went* . . . . *out* . . . . and we couldn't see a thing.

2. After a short break they . . . . with their work.

3. She . . . . six children on her own.

4. We . . . . tea and drank coffee instead.

5. She . . . . the instructions very carefully.

6. You . . . . the most important thing! You didn't tell us where we were going to meet.

7. I . . . . this letter while I was cleaning.

8. Because of her bright clothes she really . . . . from the others in the group.

B. Now do the same thing with these verbs and the words on the right.

catch	fall	hang	hold		for	out
sell	wear	set(2)			off	up

1. Some thieves . . . . the bank at lunchtime.

2. They . . . . on the excursion at 7 o'clock.

3. The bookstore . . . . of copies of his latest novel within two hours. Everybody wanted to buy it.

4. She . . . . him because he was so amusing.

5. The dinner burned and . . . . the smoke alarm.

6. She . . . . in the middle of our conversation. Maybe I said something wrong.

7. The children's new shoes . . . . so quickly that we had to buy a new pair after only two months.

8. They soon . . . . with me although I left 20 minutes before they did.

48 Shopping list

When we talk about chocolate or coffee, we can use the expressions:

a bar of chocolate   a cup of coffee

There are many other expressions like this. They help us to talk about a quantity of something. They can often be used to answer the question *How much would you like?*

Match the words on the left with the correct words on the right. Use each word once only. Write your answers in the boxes.

1.	a ball of	**a.**	bread	1	
2.	a bar of	**b.**	cards	2	
3.	a bunch of	**c.**	cigarettes	3	
4.	a jar of	**d.**	thread	4	
5.	a loaf of	**e.**	flowers	5	
6.	a book of	**f.**	matches	6	
7.	a pack of	**g.**	jam	7	
8.	a deck of	**h.**	pearls	8	
9.	a pad of	**i.**	gasoline	9	
10.	a pair of	**j.**	scissors	10	
11.	a spool of	**k.**	soap	11	
12.	a string of	**l.**	string	12	
13.	a tank of	**m.**	toothpaste	13	
14.	a tube of	**n.**	writing paper	14	

49 Sentence starters – 2

Here are three more ways of starting a sentence. Can you complete them in each situation? There is a list of phrases at the bottom of the page to help you.

Would you like....?

1. You are having a birthday party.
   Invite a friend.   Would you like.............
2. Your friend's teacup is empty.
   Offer her some more.   Would you like.............
3. Your friend is not good at numbers.
   You have a calculator.   Would you like.............
4. Your friend's suitcase looks very heavy.   Would you like.............
5. You want to learn German.
   A German friend says: Would you like.............

Let's....

6. You and some friends want to go out
   to eat. Chinese?   Let's............................
7. You are tired. You don't want to go out
   tonight.   Let's............................
8. There's nothing good on TV tonight.   Let's............................
9. You are on the beach. It is very very hot.   Let's............................
10. It is easier for you and your friends to
    go to the airport by taxi.   Let's............................

You'd better....

11. Your friend is going out. It is raining.   You'd better ....
12. Your friend has a toothache.   You'd better ....
13. Someone has just stolen your friend's car.   You'd better ....
14. Your friend wants to work in America.
    She doesn't speak much English.   You'd better ....
15. There is a lot of water on the floor in your
    friend's hotel room.   You'd better ....

Useful phrases: some more tea, carry, go for a swim, put on your raincoat, go to a Chinese restaurant, learn quickly, stay at home, me to teach you, call the dentist, rent a video, come to my party, call reception, take a taxi, borrow my calculator, phone the police.

> If you remember these sentences exactly, you can use them yourself, **and** they will help you with the patterns of the language.

50 Word partnerships – 3

Choose an adjective from the list on the left and put it with a preposition from the list on the right to complete the sentence. Use each adjective once only.

afraid	**good**	**mad**	**at**
close	**grateful**	**similar**	**for**
famous	**anxious**	**sorry**	**of**
full	**ready**	**tired**	**to**

1. She won't talk to me. Do you think she's . . . . me?

2. They live . . . . the new mall, which makes shopping easier for them.

3. I'm afraid I'm not very . . . . speaking Italian but I'll do my best.

4. I'm . . . . doing the same things all the time! Can't we do something different?

5. At night that tree is . . . . birds. The noise makes it difficult for me to get to sleep.

6. Her dress is very . . . . mine. Only the belt is different.

7. Your cousin sounds interesting. I'm . . . . meet him.

8. The town is . . . . its museum. People come from all over the world to visit it.

9. We had to go by sea because he's . . . . flying.

10. It's very kind of you. We're very . . . . all your help.

11. Aren't you . . . . the party yet? The taxi's coming in five minutes!

12. Everybody felt very . . . . him after his terrible accident.

> Remember you need to learn **word partnerships**, not just individual words. It's also easier to remember the partnerships if you learn them in whole sentences — especially if the sentences are funny or personal for you.

51 What's missing? – 2

Under each picture write the name of the item and what is missing. Choose from the following list of words.

bicycle	heel	seat
boat	jacket	sails
clock	keys	shoe
stove	piano	sleeve
dog	receiver	tail
hand	burner	telephone

1. . . . .

. . . .

2. . . . .

. . . .

3. . . . .

. . . .

4. . . . .

. . . .

5. . . . .

. . . .

6. . . . .

. . . .

7. . . . .

. . . .

8. . . . .

. . . .

9. . . . .

. . . .

52 Confusing words – 1

If you use a word in the wrong way, learn from your mistake. Find out what the correct word or expression should be and then use both the correct and incorrect words in sentences so that you can understand and remember the difference.

Choose the correct word for each sentence.

1. He's only five but he's very *big / great* for his age.
2. Could you *borrow / lend* me some money?
3. Please *bring / take* that book over here.
4. I'd like to *buy / pay* you a drink.
5. Can you *check / control* that the baby's all right?
6. You must *come / go* and visit us some time.
7. I'm a *cook / cooker* in a hotel.
8. Take your books off the bedroom *floor / ground*.
9. I think I *forgot / left* my gloves at the movies.
10. Please *hear / listen* to this carefully.
11. Short women often love *high / tall* men.
12. The dog ate *it's / its* food noisily.
13. She loves reading about the *last / latest* fashion.
14. I *passed / past* the store on the way home.
15. Be *quiet / quite!* He's trying to sleep!
16. He *saw / watched* her carefully to learn how to do it.
17. Can you *say / tell* me what he said?
18. *Who's / Whose* book is this?

When you are sure you know the correct answers, cross out the wrong ones carefully.

If you write your own sentence with the correct word, it will help you to remember how to use it.

53 Word groups – 3

Put each of the words below into the correct list. Use each word once only. Can you think of any more words to add to each list?

ballad	dime	nickel	quarter
ballot	dip	oldies	sitcom
barbecue	donut	out of shape	sit-ups
campaign	flabby	penny	soap opera
constituency	jingle	platform	sweats
deli	lullaby	prime time	talk show

TELEVISION

. . . .

. . . .

. . . .

. . . .

FOOD

. . . .

. . . .

. . . .

. . . .

ELECTIONS

. . . .

. . . .

. . . .

. . . .

U.S. CURRENCY

. . . .

. . . .

. . . .

. . . .

MUSIC

. . . .

. . . .

. . . .

. . . .

FITNESS & HEALTH

. . . .

. . . .

. . . .

. . . .

54 Complaining

Can I help you?

I hope so. I bought a . . . . here last week. Unfortunately,

. . . .

Match the items with what is wrong with them.

1.	book	**a.**	The playing instructions are missing.
2.	camera	**b.**	It's color, not black and white.
3.	film	**c.**	It rewinds cassettes very slowly.
4.	game	**d.**	It loses time.
5.	guitar	**e.**	The heel came off one of them the first time I wore them.
6.	pair of scissors	**f.**	It stretched when I washed it.
7.	pair of shoes	**g.**	Two of its strings are broken.
8.	pen	**h.**	It has a scratch on its lens.
9.	radio	**i.**	Some keys don't work properly.
10.	sweater	**j.**	Some pages are missing.
11.	tape recorder	**k.**	It doesn't write properly.
12.	kettle	**l.**	The antenna is broken.
13.	typewriter	**m.**	It doesn't have a lid.
14.	watch	**n.**	They don't cut properly.

1	2	3	4	5	6	7	8	9	10	11	12	13	14

Write your answers here:

Can you think of any other things which could go wrong with these items?

55 Clothes – 2

Think about the clothes you wear. Look at pictures of clothes in newspapers and magazines. Do you know what to call them in English? If not find out.

Why don't you make your own picture dictionary? Cut out pictures of clothes, stick them in a book and put their names in English next to them. This will help you to remember things better.

Can you name the 16 things Korky is wearing? Use each of these once:

boot	belt	coat	necklace
shoe	tie	goggles	brooch
glove	shirt	crown	zipper
pullover	crash helmet	umbrella	sock

16. _____

15. _____

14. _____

13. _____

12. _____

1. _____

2. _____

3. _____

4. _____

5. _____

6. _____

7. _____

8. _____

9. _____

10. _____

11. _____

56 Word partnerships – 4

Match the verb on the left with a noun on the right. Use each word once only. Write your answers in the boxes.

Set 1

1.	boil	**a.**	a bell	**1**	
2.	brush	**b.**	an egg	**2**	
3.	cross	**c.**	a hole	**3**	
4.	dig	**d.**	a jacket	**4**	
5.	organize	**e.**	a letter	**5**	
6.	mail	**f.**	money	**6**	
7.	ring	**g.**	a party	**7**	
8.	spell	**h.**	a road	**8**	
9.	spend	**i.**	your teeth	**9**	
10.	wear	**j.**	a word	**10**	

Set 2

1.	answer	**a.**	a cake	**1**	
2.	bake	**b.**	the car	**2**	
3.	blow	**c.**	a carpet	**3**	
4.	earn	**d.**	a horse	**4**	
5.	lay	**e.**	your name	**5**	
6.	park	**f.**	your nose	**6**	
7.	play	**g.**	the phone	**7**	
8.	ride	**h.**	the piano	**8**	
9.	sign	**i.**	a pipe	**9**	
10.	smoke	**j.**	a salary	**10**	

57 Animal world – 1

Under each picture write the name of the creature.
Choose from the following list of words.

elephant   **ostrich**   **lion**   **owl**
crab   **mouse**   **penguin**   **crocodile**
giraffe   **bear**   **rhinoceros**   **frog**

1. . . . .   2. . . . .   3. . . . .

4. . . . .   5. . . . .   6. . . . .

7. . . . .   8. . . . .   9. . . . .

10. . . . .   11. . . . .   12. . . . .

58 Replace the word

Don't immediately look up every word you don't know. Try to guess the meaning by what goes before and after it and then, if necessary, check in a dictionary to see if you're right.

Complete each sentence by using a more common word than the word in parentheses, for example:

He usually comes by bus but *sometimes* he comes by taxi. (OCCASIONALLY)

1. I can't carry this by myself. Could somebody . . . . me? (ASSIST)

2. They . . . . to speak to him but they didn't succeed. (ATTEMPTED)

3. Slowly and . . . . he carried the glasses outside. (CAUTIOUSLY)

4. She . . . . the money under the bed so that nobody would find it. (CONCEALED)

5. They're . . . . a new apartment building near the park. (CONSTRUCTING)

6. The table was too . . . . to get through the door. (ENORMOUS)

7. He used to visit me every day but he doesn't come so . . . . these days. (FREQUENTLY)

8. She . . . . about flights to Rio but they didn't have any information. (INQUIRED)

9. The machine isn't working very well. It . . . . some more oil. (REQUIRES)

10. I got no . . . . when I asked how old she was. (RESPONSE)

11. The police are still . . . . for the boy who ran away. (SEARCHING)

12. It was difficult to . . . . a winner because they were all so good. (SELECT)

13. She did it so . . . . that she finished in 30 minutes. (SPEEDILY)

14. I'm not . . . . enough to buy a car as big as his. (WEALTHY)

59 Rooms of the house – 2

Remember to use what you have around you to learn English. Look at the things you have around you at home and see if you know how to say them in English. If you don't know, find out.

Look at the picture of a kitchen. On the list below, number each item which is numbered on the picture.

. . . . shelf	. . . . stove	. . . . dish towel
. . . . mixer	. . . . oven	. . . . table cloth
. . . . sink	. . . . teapot	. . . . pitcher
. . . . faucet	. . . . pot	. . . . bowl

60 Word formation – 3

Change the word to complete the sentence, for example:

There was a lot of . *activity* . in the room. (ACTIVE)

1. It's hard to find . . . . in the summer. (ACCOMMODATE)

2. She has a large . . . . of stamps. (COLLECT)

3. He made an unfavorable . . . . between food in his country and mine. (COMPARE)

4. They made a . . . . about the heating. (COMPLAIN)

5. I had to write a . . . . for homework. (COMPOSE)

6. She gave a . . . . of the new computer. (DEMONSTRATE)

7. I had . . . . starting my car this morning. (DIFFICULT)

8. Do you have some kind of . . . . on you? (IDENTIFY)

9. How serious is her . . . . ? (ILL)

10. They had a very happy . . . . (MARRY)

11. There was a strange . . . . in the bowl. (MIX)

12. Gardening is a relaxing . . . . for some people, but not for me! (OCCUPY)

13. Could I have . . . . to go home early? (PERMIT)

14. There are several . . . . mistakes in this letter. (PUNCTUATE)

15. I have made a . . . . for next weekend. (RESERVE)

16. He made a . . . . about the robbery. (STATE)

17. He made another . . . . about who to invite. (SUGGEST)

18. Can I get a . . . . of this book? (TRANSLATE)

19. He's getting . . . . for his bad back. (TREAT)

20. I've put on . . . . since I arrived here. (WEIGH)

70

61 Two-word expressions

Sometimes in English two words are used together to make a common expression, for example:

credit card   vacuum cleaner

Sometimes you find these expressions listed separately in a dictionary and sometimes they are included in the definitions of one, or both, of the two words. You need to learn the expressions as complete phrases.

Join one word on the left with one from the right to make a two-word partnership. Use each word once only. Write your answers in the boxes.

1.	parking	a.	agency	1	
2.	department	b.	field	2	
3.	departure	c.	house	3	
4.	movie	d.	juice	4	
5.	football	e.	lights	5	
6.	guest	f.	lounge	6	
7.	luggage	g.	money	7	
8.	orange	h.	office	8	
9.	gas	i.	lot	9	
10.	pocket	j.	pool	10	
11.	post	k.	processor	11	
12.	swimming	l.	rack	12	
13.	traffic	m.	star	13	
14.	travel	n.	station	14	
15.	windshield	o.	store	15	
16.	word	p.	wipers	16	

Now complete each sentence with one of the expressions.

1.   He put the suitcases up on the . . . .

2.   They went shopping in a big . . . .

3.   She bought a . . . . to replace her typewriter.

4.   Is there any more . . . .? I'm very thirsty.

71

62 Sports and hobbies

Match the sport or hobby on the left with the item you use on the right.
Use each item once only. Write your answers in the boxes.

1.	bird-watching	**a.**	bat	1	
2.	boxing	**b.**	bicycle	2	
3.	camping	**c.**	binoculars	3	
4.	canoeing	**d.**	brush	4	
5.	cycling	**e.**	club	5	
6.	fishing	**f.**	film	6	
7.	football	**g.**	gloves	7	
8.	gardening	**h.**	helmet	8	
9.	golf	**i.**	needles	9	
10.	hockey	**j.**	paddle	10	
11.	knitting	**k.**	racket	11	
12.	painting	**l.**	rod	12	
13.	photography	**m.**	saw	13	
14.	baseball	**n.**	shovel	14	
15.	tennis	**o.**	stick	15	
16.	woodwork	**p.**	tent	16	

Now match the correct pair with each of the pictures below.

Can you think of any more things you need if you are interested in these
sports and hobbies?

63 Expressions with 'll

Match up what you think (in the left hand bubbles) with what you actually say in the right hand bubbles.

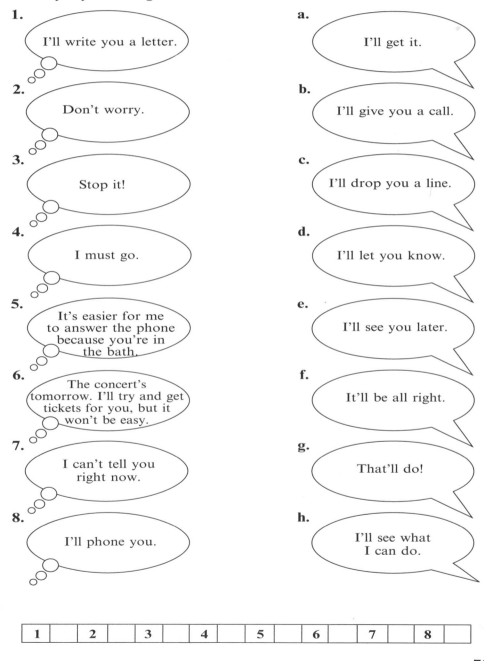

1. I'll write you a letter.

a. I'll get it.

2. Don't worry.

b. I'll give you a call.

3. Stop it!

c. I'll drop you a line.

4. I must go.

d. I'll let you know.

5. It's easier for me to answer the phone because you're in the bath.

e. I'll see you later.

6. The concert's tomorrow. I'll try and get tickets for you, but it won't be easy.

f. It'll be all right.

7. I can't tell you right now.

g. That'll do!

8. I'll phone you.

h. I'll see what I can do.

1		2		3		4		5		6		7		8	

64 Word partnerships – 5

Remember to keeping noting pairs of words which often occur together. This can help you to understand English because if you see or hear one of them, you can **expect** the other.

Match the adjective on the left with a noun on the right. Use each word once only. Write your answers in the boxes.

Set 1

1.	crowded	**a.**	accident	1	
2.	dark	**b.**	bed	2	
3.	deep	**c.**	bus	3	
4.	fair	**d.**	climate	4	
5.	fatal	**e.**	cloud	5	
6.	flat	**f.**	difficulty	6	
7.	great	**g.**	food	7	
8.	mild	**h.**	hair	8	
9.	single	**i.**	river	9	
10.	tasty	**j.**	tire	10	

Set 2

Now do the same with these words

1.	amateur	**a.**	bottle	1	
2.	bright	**b.**	bread	2	
3.	busy	**c.**	ceremony	3	
4.	embarrassing	**d.**	color	4	
5.	empty	**e.**	hotel	5	
6.	high	**f.**	mountain	6	
7.	luxury	**g.**	photographer	7	
8.	religious	**h.**	question	8	
9.	sliced	**i.**	fog	9	
10.	thick	**j.**	street	10	

65 Word formation – 4

Change the word to complete the sentence, for example:

It was very . *misty* . . this morning. (MIST)

1. Artists are often . . . . about their work. (PASSION)

2. It was too . . . . for sunbathing. (CLOUD)

3. The room got so . . . . that he had to clean it. (DUST)

4. It was . . . . not to write down the address. (FOOL)

5. The receptionist was very . . . . and explained everything to him very carefully. (HELP)

6. You were . . . . not to be killed. (LUCK)

7. She lives in a very . . . . apartment. (LUXURY)

8. I had to have a . . . . examination before they gave me the job. (MEDICINE)

9. He slipped on the . . . . ground. (MUD)

10. What was that . . . . buzzing sound? (MYSTERY)

11. He was very . . . . before his interview. (NERVE)

12. I prefer the . . . . version of this movie. (ORIGIN)

13. She got a . . . . letter from her boss. (PERSON)

14. Some . . . . singers earn a lot of money. (PROFESSION)

15. We bought this house at a very . . . . price. (REASON)

16. I think the most . . . . idea is to go by car. (SENSE)

17. The soldier had very . . . . boots. (SHINE)

18. She was very kind and . . . . when I told her about my problem. (SYMPATHY)

19. There are . . . . ways of doing this. (VARY)

20. It was too . . . . to use my umbrella. (WIND)

75

66 Product information

If you can get newspapers or magazines in English, look at the advertisements. You can find a lot of useful vocabulary in them.
In addition, many products have information written in English which will also help you to build your vocabulary.
Remember, there are lots of opportunities to see real English. All of them can help you to learn.

In this exercise you will see information about a product. It is from information or a label on the product.
You have to decide which product. Choose the product from the following list:

bookcase	medicine	sheet
coffee	newspaper	socks
film	paint	television
kettle	ring	pants
marmalade	shampoo	watch

THICK CUT *made from Seville* *oranges*	**TO FIT** **DOUBLE BED**	Helps clear a stuffed or runny nose

1. . . . . 2. . . . . 3. . . . .

FILTER FINE *MEDIUM ROAST*	**FOR NORMAL** **HAIR**	Business 40-43 Gardening 50 TV Guide 52

4. . . . . 5. . . . . 6. . . . .

WAIST 36in	**FOR COLOR PRINTS**	**TO FIT SHOE SIZES 6-10**

7. . . . .   8. . . . .   9. . . . .

FOR CEILINGS AND WALLS	LOOP ANTENNA 30 CHANNELS	**4 SHELVES**

10. . . . .   11. . . . .   12. . . . .

Rapidly boils up to 3 pints of water	*With 15 rubies and 4 diamonds*	**Time, date. Alarm. Stop-watch.**

13. . . . .   14. . . . .   15. . . . .

Look again at page 11. Cover the words at the top of the page. Look at the pictures for one minute. Now write down as many of the words as you can remember, without looking at the picutre again. Remember, looking **back** and revising what you have already learned is an important part of building your vocabulary.

67 Confusing words – 2

If you use a word in the wrong way, learn from your mistake. Find out what the correct word or expression should be then use both the correct and incorrect words in sentences so that you can understand and remember the difference.

Choose the correct word for each sentence.

1.   What would you *advice / advise* me to do?
2.   The train has been *delayed / postponed* ten minutes.
3.   He's the person who *discovered / invented* television.
4.   We *wait for / expect* him to arrive tomorrow morning.
5.   That color doesn't *fit / suit* you.
6.   He's a complete *foreigner / stranger*. I've never seen him before.
7.   His favorite *game / play* is football.
8.   I'm pleased everybody has worked so *hard / hardly*.
9.   He's starting a new *job / work* on Monday.
10.   He's going to *lay / lie* on the bed and rest.
11.   When you arrive in town, go to the *nearest / next* police station.
12.   She left a *note / notice* on the kitchen table to tell him where she was.
13.   Did you *notice / remark* what he was wearing?
14.   She *passed / took* the exam in July but she won't know the result before October.
15.   They won the first *price / prize* in the competition.
16.   Could you *remember / remind* me to phone her?
17.   The accident happened on the *road / street* from Burlingame to Concord.
18.   They *robbed / stole* the money from the house last night.

When you are sure you know the correct answers, cross out the wrong ones.

Don't forget that if you write your own sentences, it will help you to remember how to use the words correctly.

68 Animal world – 2

Under each picture write the name of the creature.
Choose from the following list of words.

pig	**monkey**	**zebra**	**shark**
horse	**snake**	**parrot**	**bull**
rabbit	**squirrel**	**tortoise**	**deer**

1. . . . .

2. . . . .

3. . . . .

4. . . . .

5. . . . .

6. . . . .

7. . . . .

8. . . . .

9. . . . .

10. . . . .

11. . . . .

12. . . . .

69 Guess the subject

In most countries, it is possible to receive radio programs in English. Listening to the news and other programs will help you improve your English.

If you don't hear or don't understand everything, don't worry. It is often possible to guess what people are talking about because you hear other words that go very closely with a subject. For example, if you hear the words:

sweater, right size, expensive, overcoat

the people are probably talking about buying clothes.

What is 'it' in each of these sentences? The words in italics should help you to guess. Write your answer in the space provided.

1. It *shone brightly* all day and made the room very *warm*. . . . .
2. The *artist* took 2 months to *paint* it. . . . .
3. She heard it *ringing* and ran into the room to *answer* it. . . . .
4. It isn't *sharp* enough to *cut* the vegetables. . . . .
5. It was so *strong* that it *blew down* that tree. . . . .
6. He *kicked* it past the *keeper* into the *goal*. . . . .
7. It *fell heavily* and made all the countryside *white*. . . . .
8. My *dentist* said it needed a *filling*. . . . .
9. It *expires* next month so I have to get a new one before I *go abroad again*. . . . .
10. It leaves from *platform 3* at seven fifteen. . . . .
11. I've *taken* some very good *pictures* with it. . . . .
12. It's the one I usually *borrow books from*. . . . .
13. I sometimes need it to *look up words I don't understand* . . . .
14. He *turned* it *on* but didn't really *watch* it until the news came on. . . . .

70 Compound nouns

Sometimes in English it is possible to join two separate words together to make one noun, for example:

tooth   **brush**   **toothbrush**   **hand bag**   **handbag**

These are another kind of 'word partnership' which you have already met several times in this book. These combinations are very important if you want your English to be natural.

Join one word from the group on the left, and one from the group on the right to make compound nouns. Use each word once only. Write your answers in the boxes.

1.	book	a.	paper		1	
2.	foot	b.	ball		2	
3.	girl	c.	way		3	
4.	hair	d.	card		4	
5.	home	e.	case		5	
6.	key	f.	coat		6	
7.	sofa	g.	dryer		7	
8.	news	h.	fall		8	
9.	post	i.	friend		9	
10.	rain	j.	hole		10	
11.	shoe	k.	lace		11	
12.	sign	l.	paste		12	
13.	head	m.	post		13	
14.	tooth	n.	light		14	
15.	free	o.	bed		15	
16.	water	p.	work		16	

Now complete each sentence with one of the compound nouns.

1. Our teacher gives us too much . . . . to do.

2. It's much quicker if you travel on the . . . .

3. If there aren't enough beds, we can use the . . . .

4. Send me a . . . . while you're in Japan!

81

71 Things used at work – 2

Match each person with the thing she/he uses at work. Use each item once only. Write your answers in the boxes.

1.	actor/actress	a.	wire	1	
2.	paramedic	b.	computer	2	
3.	announcer	c.	crash helmet	3	
4.	artist	d.	easel	4	
5.	astronomer	e.	handcuffs	5	
6.	doctor	f.	hose	6	
7.	dress-maker	g.	make-up	7	
8.	electrician	h.	microphone	8	
9.	fireman	i.	notebook	9	
10.	florist	j.	saddle	10	
11.	jockey	k.	sewing-machine	11	
12.	journalist	l.	stethoscope	12	
13.	plumber	m.	stretcher	13	
14.	policeman/woman	n.	faucet	14	
15.	programmer	o.	telescope	15	
16.	racing driver	p.	vase	16	

Now match the correct pair with each of the pictures below.

Can you think of any more things the people could use?

72 Opposites – prefixes

You can form the opposite of some adjectives by using a prefix, for example:

certain   **un**certain

In this word square, find fourteen adjectives formed in this way. The words can go across or down, or diagonally left to right. The same letter may be used in more than one word. The prefixes used are **im-**, **in-** or **un-**. One has been done for you as an example.

```
U  N  N  E  C  E  S  S  A  R  Y  U
U  N  U  S  U  A  L  O  U  I  I  N
N  A  P  H  A  L  L  O  N  N  N  F
A  U  N  L  U  C  K  Y  T  C  D  R
B  X  H  E  E  D  O  N  I  O  E  I
L  O  N  N  A  E  W  E  M  P  E
E  O  F  I  N  I  S  K  D  P  E  N
R  N  K  I  T  E  K  A  P  L  N  D
U  N  H  A  P  P  Y  O  N  E  D  L
U  M  P  I  M  P  O  L  I  T  E  Y
I  M  P  O  S  S  I  B  L  E  N  N
I  N  C  O  R  R  E  C  T  Y  T  O
```

Now find the best word from the word square to complete each of the following sentences.

1.   It's very . . . . to have snow in the middle of summer.
2.   After 100 years as a colony the country became . . . .
3.   Careful you don't trip! Your shoelaces are . . . .
4.   He's . . . . to see you at the moment. He's very busy.
5.   You will lose one point for each . . . . answer.
6.   It's . . . . to reach the town. The roads are blocked.

73 Horrible joke time

Different people find different things funny.

Here are some examples of jokes which some people find quite amusing. (Other people think they are just silly.)

Match the question on the left with the answer on the right.

1.	What is the longest word in the English language?	a.	A tomato in an elevator.
2.	What time is it when an elephant sits on your watch?	b.	A roof.
3.	What kind of umbrella does a teacher carry on a rainy day?	c.	The smallest ones.
4.	Which fish have got their eyes closest together?	d.	A person on a horse.
5.	What do you call little white things in your head which bite?	e.	Smiles – there's a mile between the two Ss.
6.	What's the difference between here and there?	f.	So that he could be on time.
7.	What's red and goes up and down?	g.	A wet one.
8.	Why do white sheep eat more than black sheep?	h.	May — it only has 3 letters.
9.	Why did the student sit on his watch?	i.	Lunch and dinner.
10.	What goes up but never comes down?	j.	The letter T.
11.	What 2 things shouldn't you have before breakfast?	k.	There are more of them.
12.	What do you find all over a house?	l.	Your age.
13.	What has 6 legs, 2 arms and 2 heads?	m.	Time to buy a new one.
14.	Which is the shortest month?	n.	Teeth.

Write your answers here:

1	2	3	4	5	6	7	8	9	10	11	12	13	14

74 Expressions with 'not'

In English it can often seem rude to answer with the one word 'No'. Each of the expressions in the right hand column is a natural response using 'not'. Match up the remarks in the left-hand column with those on the right to make natural conversations.

1. Did you enjoy the book?	a. **Not again**.
2. Some coffee?	b. **Not exactly**. My Spanish is better.
3. Somebody's been smoking in here!	c. **Not likely**! I'm scared of flying!
4. They're raising interest rates.	d. **Not very many**. About 10.
5. Are you ready to go out?	e. **Not right now, thanks**. I've just had lunch.
6. Are you bilingual?	f. **Not really**. I had to work on Saturday.
7. Would you like something to eat?	g. **Not for me, thanks**. I prefer tea.
8. Did you have a good weekend?	h. **Not yet**. Give me 5 minutes.
9. How many people were at the party?	i. **Not me**!
10. Are you coming paragliding with us?	j. **Not a whole lot**. It was too long.

1		2		3		4		5		6		7		8		9		10	

Now respond with one of the expressions using 'not' to the following:

11. Would you like some candy?	.... , ...
12. Someone took my pen!	....!
13. Did you have a good flight?	....
14. What've you been doing?	....
15. I suppose you bought a lot of books!	....

Remember, your English will sound more natural if you can use these fixed expressions.

Test 1 Units 1–15

Choose the best word to complete each sentence.

1. Excuse me. Could you . . . . me the way to the town hall?
    a. let   **b.** put   **c.** talk   **d.** tell

2. Not more books! There aren't enough . . . . to put them on!
    a. leaves   **b.** cases   **c.** spaces   **d.** shelves

3. Don't forget your . . . . It's very cold outside.
    a. gloves   **b.** socks   **c.** umbrella   **d.** scissors

4. There are eleven players in a soccer . . . .
    a. game   **b.** pitch   **c.** team   **d.** group

5. What's wrong with your foot? – One of my . . . . hurts.
    a. fingers   **b.** heels   **c.** wrists   **d.** toes

6. Bill's a . . . . so he travels all over the world.
    a. baker   **b.** butcher   **c.** sailor   **d.** driver

7. The . . . . will help you if you can't find the book you want.
    a. porter   **b.** agent   **c.** librarian   **d.** operator

8. I must reserve a . . . . for our game of tennis tomorrow.
    a. field   **b.** court   **c.** green   **d.** team

9. My car won't start. Could you give me a . . . . to town?
    a. bus   **b.** car   **c.** hand   **d.** lift

10. Do you take . . . . in your coffee?
    a. spoon   **b.** pepper   **c.** salt   **d.** sugar

11. This doll is a present for my . . . . I hope she likes it.
    a. husband   **b.** nephew   **c.** niece   **d.** uncle

12. What kind of fruit would you like? – A . . . . , please.
    a. carrot   **b.** mushroom   **c.** pear   **d.** turnip

13. I'll look in my . . . . and see if I'm free on Wednesday.
    a. calendar   **b.** dictionary   **c.** briefcase   **d.** purse

14. You don't have to . . . . ! We're not late!
    a. dream   **b.** laugh   **c.** rush   **d.** wait

15. Which do you . . . . – cream or milk?
    a. rather   **b.** eat   **c.** prefer   **d.** wear

Test 2 Units 16–30

Choose the best word to complete each sentence.

1. You can hang your jacket in the . . . .
   a. bedspread   b. dresser   c. hanger   d. closet
2. It doesn't . . . . much difference whether we finish today or not.
   a. pay   b. show   c. do   d. make
3. Could you . . . . a picture of me in front of this building?
   a. check   b. make   c. do   d. take
4. The ice is very . . . . so don't walk on it.
   a. high   b. low   c. thick   d. thin
5. Carol speaks so fast that it's . . . . to understand her.
   a. difficult   b. easy   c. slow   d. wrong
6. The mechanic hopes to . . . . our car by this evening.
   a. make   b. renew   c. repair   d. wander
7. My . . . . says I need stronger glasses.
   a. pharmacist   b. conductor   c. keeper   d. optician
8. Can I pay you tomorrow? – That's fine . . . . me.
   a. about   b. by   c. of   d. to
9. How much does she earn? – That's none of your . . . . !
   a. business   b. decision   c. information   d. role
10. The police are looking for the . . . . of a red Mustang.
    a. detective   b. instructor   c. owner   d. rider
11. I've already got a . . . . at a hotel near the convention center.
    a. book   b. property   c. reserve   d. reservation
12. The next . . . . of the show is at seven thirty.
    a. event   b. performance   c. stall   d. game
13. You can't eat that pear. It isn't . . . . yet.
    a. best   b. pale   c. ripe   d. mature
14. Can you . . . . the coffee and I'll get the cookies.
    a. depart   b. disturb   c. feed   d. pour
15. Should I wear my sandals or my . . . . ?
    a. sweater   b. shorts   c. sneakers   d. scarves

Test 3 Units 31–45

Choose the best alternative to complete each sentence.

1. Shirley tried to stop the car but the . . . . didn't work.
   a. brakes **b.** crossroads **c.** tires **d.** controls
2. The referee and the two teams ran out onto the . . . .
   a. circus **b.** course **c.** observatory **d.** field
3. You need some . . . . coffee to wake you up.
   a. awake **b.** hard **c.** brown **d.** strong
4. His suitcase was pretty . . . . so I could easily carry it.
   a. cheap **b.** heavy **c.** light **d.** short
5. When did you . . . . smoking? – About two years ago.
   a. cut off **b.** give up **c.** make up **d.** throw away
6. The plane . . . . late because of the terrible weather.
   a. blew up **b.** grew up **c.** went on **d.** took off
7. The . . . . at the hospital told me not to worry about my leg.
   a. accountant **b.** director **c.** lodger **d.** specialist
8. The President is a very . . . . man. Everyone does what he says.
   a. circular **b.** direct **c.** painful **d.** powerful
9. We had to . . . . the match because of the bad weather.
   a. call back **b.** call off **c.** think over **d.** find out
10. Pat was surprised when her boss didn't . . . . the meal.
    a. buy **b.** pay **c.** pay for **d.** spend
11. All Michael ate was two thin . . . . of bread.
    a. rolls **b.** loaves **c.** slices **d.** snacks
12. With this . . . . I can get to the windows on the first floor.
    a. index **b.** ladder **c.** lager **d.** step
13. You can . . . . a bus just outside the station.
    a. beat **b.** catch **c.** keep **d.** meet
14. Take your overcoat with you . . . . it gets cold.
    a. although **b.** in case **c.** unless **d.** until
15. I'd like to . . . . this check, please.
    a. cash **b.** change **c.** pay for **d.** spend

Test 4 Units 46–59

Choose the best alternative to complete each sentence.

1. Suddenly there was a loud bang and the lights . . . .
    a. did without   **b.** caught up   **c.** went out   **d.** wore out
2. Jimmy sent his mother a . . . . of flowers for her birthday.
    a. bar   **b.** bunch   **c.** pack   **d.** packet
3. It's raining. . . . . take your umbrella with you.
    a. Are you going   **b.** Let's   **c.** You'd better   **d.** Would you like
4. There's nothing good on television. Let's . . . . a video.
    a. carry   **b.** rent   **c.** invite   **d.** phone
5. Can't you do it? I'm not very good . . . . explaining things.
    a. at   **b.** for   **c.** of   **d.** to
6. Thanks very much! I'm very . . . . for your help.
    a. generous   **b.** grateful   **c.** full   **d.** sorry
7. I like the color of the jacket but the . . . . are too short.
    a. buttons   **b.** heels   **c.** collars   **d.** sleeves
8. Can you just . . . . that all the windows are shut?
    a. catch   **b.** check   **c.** control   **d.** reclaim
9. Which . . . . does our flight leave from? – Number 12.
    a. carriageway   **b.** exit   **c.** gate   **d.** ground
10. Look at my sweater! It . . . . when I washed it.
    a. boiled   **b.** cut   **c.** missed   **d.** stretched
11. Wear a . . . . to protect your head in case there's an
    accident.
    a. brooch   **b.** crash helmet   **c.** glove   **d.** cap
12. Could you . . . . your name at the bottom of the letter?
    a. answer   **b.** cross   **c.** lay   **d.** sign
13. James is a terrible cook. He can't even . . . . an egg!
    a. blow   **b.** boil   **c.** lay   **d.** smoke
14. Surely they aren't . . . . enough to buy such a large car!
    a. cautious   **b.** well   **c.** poor   **d.** wealthy
15. There isn't any water coming out of this . . . .
    a. heel   **b.** lock   **c.** shelf   **d.** faucet

Test 5 Units 60–74

Choose the best alternative to complete each sentence.

1. I've put on . . . . I eat too many cakes.
   a. gloves   **b.** mixture   **c.** waist   **d.** weight
2. Put your suitcase up on the luggage . . . .
   a. lounge   **b.** park   **c.** rack   **d.** store
3. You could hear the crowd shouting in the local football . . . .
   a. stadium   **b.** park   **c.** pool   **d.** station
4. That'll . . . ., children! Stop shouting!
   a. do   **b.** fit   **c.** help   **d.** make
5. I can't tell you now. I'll . . . . you know later.
   a. get   **b.** let   **c.** make   **d.** tell
6. Give me a . . . . some time. You know my phone number.
   a. date   **b.** line   **c.** post   **d.** call
7. The bus was so . . . . that we couldn't all get on.
   a. crowded   **b.** deep   **c.** thick   **d.** various
8. We have a . . . . climate so the winters are never very cold.
   a. bright   **b.** fair   **c.** high   **d.** mild
9. It's so . . . . in here. Don't you ever clean this room?
   a. cloudy   **b.** dark   **c.** dusty   **d.** misty
10. If you ask a . . . . price for your car, I'm sure you'll sell it.
    a. helpful   **b.** mild   **c.** reasonable   **d.** shiny
11. No, don't wear blue. It doesn't . . . . you.
    a. fit   **b.** notice   **c.** suit   **d.** take
12. The . . . . climbed up the tree and we couldn't see it any more.
    a. deer   **b.** rabbit   **c.** squirrel   **d.** tortoise
13. Make sure the knife is really . . . . before you cut the meat.
    a. flat   **b.** sharp   **c.** sliced   **d.** thick
14. The police put . . . . on the robbers to stop them from getting away.
    a. handcuffs   **b.** make-up   **c.** saddles   **d.** stretchers
15. Are you ready to go? – Not . . . . Give me 10 minutes.
    a. for me   **b.** very much   **c.** very many   **d.** yet

Answers

1 A 1.about 2.above 3.accent 4.act 5.action 6.active 7.actor 8.car 9.card   10.carrot
B lid   **C** light a cigarette, paint a picture, park a car, write a letter   **D** nationality, national, difference, different   **E** came, went, paid, saw, stopped   **F** wear, south

2 1.start 2.tell 3.let 4.thank 5.knock 6.keep 7.put 8.take 9.end 10.do 11.order 12.read 13.dream 14.meet 15.talk 16.kiss

3 1.last month 2.a couple of weeks ago 3.last Friday 4.last weekend 5.the day before yesterday 6.yesterday morning 7.yesterday afternoon 8.today 9.tomorrow 10.the day after tomorrow 11.next weekend 12.next Tuesday 13.a week from tomorrow 14.three weeks from now

4 A. a.addresses b.boxes c.boys d.children e.knives f.leaves g.stories h.men i.potatoes j.tomatoes k.watches l.women   **B**. 1.sandwiches 2.teeth 3.days 4.beaches 5.countries 6.shelves 7.feet 8.dresses

5 1.arrow 2.bird 3.boat 4.bottle 5.envelope 6.fork 7.glasses 8.scissors 9.pear 10.razor 11.gloves 12.puddle 13.spoon 14.umbrella 15.parachute 16.tree 17.hairbrush 18.mushroom 19.ring 20.robot

6 1.eleven 2.ten 3.twenty 4.seven 5.fifteen 6.hundred 7.three 8.five 9.twelve 10.seventy 11.eight 12.seventy-seven 13.thirty-three 14.fifty-six or sixty-six 15.fifty-five or sixty-five

7 1.ear 2.neck 3.elbow 4.finger 5.stomach 6.foot 7.toe 8.heel 9.leg 10.hand 11.chest 12.arm 13.shoulder 14.tongue 15.mouth 16.eye

8 1.artist 2.baker 3.cashier 4.pharmacist 5.dancer 6.driver 7.drummer 8.electrician 9.engineer 10.gardener 11.writer 12.librarian 13.manager 14.musician 15.operator 16.painter 17.photographer 18.pianist 19.sailor 20.editor

9 1.Could I have the menu, please? 2.Could I have the fish? 3.Could I borrow a pen? 4.Could I open a window? 5.Could I try it on? 6.Could you speak up? 7.Could you turn it down? 8.Could you help me? 9.Could you give me a lift? 10.Could you tell me the way to the post office? 11.I'd like a single room, please. 12.I'd like a table for three. 13.I'd like to change some money. 14.I'd like to reserve a court. 15.I'd like an early flight.

10 1.brown, green, orange, purple 2.Friday, Saturday, Sunday, Wednesday 3.December, February, May, October 4.eight, nineteen, seventy, twelve 5.fall, spring, summer, winter 6.rain, snow, sun, wind

11 1.loser 2.baker 3.order 4.floor 5.chair 6.clear 7.river 8.sugar 9.never

12 1.husband 2.mother 3.mother-in-law 4.father 5.father-in-law 6.daughter 7.son 8.daughter-in-law 9.son-in-law 10.grandfather 11.grandmother 12.granddaughter 13.grandson 14.niece 15.nephew 16.uncle 17.aunt 18.cousin

13 1.apple 2.apricot 3.potato 4.carrot 5.coconut 6.orange 7.lemon 8.cucumber 9.melon 10.grapefruit 11.banana 12.lettuce 13.pear 14.pineapple 15.celery 16.mushroom

14 1.calendar, dictionary, envelope, notebook, pen, pencil, ruler, stamp, telephone, typewriter 2.bowl, cup, dish, fork, glass, pitcher, plate, saucer, spoon, napkin 1.ruler 2.pitcher 3.telephone 4.dictionary 5.spoon 6.envelope

15 1.rush 2.hear 3.run 4.need 5.drive 6.eat 7.throw 8.wear 9.read 10.drink 11.know 12.wait 13.travel 14.laugh 15.help 16.prefer

16 1.cabbage, music, palace, garden 2.arrive, belong, explain, guitar 3.luxury, origin, photograph, sympathy 4.arrival, mechanic, musician, successful 5.calculator, centimeter, difficulty, supermarket 6.librarian, luxurious, original, photographer

17 1.curtain 2.lamp 3.hair brush 4.lipstick 5.dresser 6.comb 7.hot water bottle 8.bedspread 9.hair dryer 10.sheet 11.coat hanger 12.pyjamas 13.pillow 14.alarm clock 15.closet 16.mirror

18 1.c 2.d 3.b 4.c 5.a 6.b 7.b 8.c 9.b 10.a 11.b 12.c

19 1.good 2.small 3.light 4.easy 5.clean 6.wet 7.slow 8.low 9.cold 10.old 11.loud 12.poor 13.tall 14.open 15.thin 16.right

20 1.b 2.d 3.b 4.c 5.a 6.c 7.b 8.a 9.a 10.b 11.a 12.d 13.c 14.a

21 1.c 2.b 3.a 4.d 5.g 6.f 7.h 8.e

22 1.announcer 2.boxer 3.criminal 4.detective 5.foreigner 6.instructor 7.inventor 8.leader 9.magician 10.writer 11.owner 12.politician 13.reporter 14.rider 15.robber 16.scientist 17.student 18.visitor

23 1.d 2.a 3.k 4.b 5.g 6.m 7.e 8.f 9.l 10.c 11.i 12.j 13.h 14.n

24 1.a park 2.outside a hotel bedroom 3.a bookstore 4.a supermarket 5.a bank 6.a football field 7.a gas station 8.an airport 9.a phone booth 10.a train 11.a hotel restaurant 12.a theater 13.a mail box 14.a children's playground 15.a zoo

25 1.clear, 2.sure 3.wish 4.while 5.tracks 6.ends 7.most 8.sick 9.tails 10.big 11.deal 12.it 13.big deal 14.difference 15.sense 16.amends

26 2.pitcher,handle 3.house,roof 4.teapot,lid 5.jacket,button 6.table,leg 7.armchair,arm 8.car,wheel 9.airplane,wing

27 1.arrival 2.competition 3.decision 4.departure 5.dictation 6.entertainment 7.equipment 8.explanation 9.expression 10.freezer 11.information 12.introduction 13.invitation 14.meeting 15.painting 16.photography 17.pronunciation 18.shopping

28 2.ripe 3.rope 4.role 5.pole 6.pale 7.pile 8.file 9.mile 10.milk 11.mill 12.fill 13.will 14.wall 15.walk 16.talk 17.tall

29 Set 1 1.h 2.f 3.e 4.c 5.i 6.g 7.d 8.a 9.b 10.j   Set 2 1.d 2.c 3.g 4.j 5.b 6.a 7.h 8.i 9.f 10.e

30 1.cap 2.scarf 3.bra 4.vest 5.shorts 6.apron 7.shoelace 8.sneaker 9.sandal 10.sweater
11.T-shirt 12.bow tie

31 1.cat, cow, feed, lion 2.brake, headlight, steer, tire 3.bird watching, knitting,
photography, stamp collecting 4.cash, check book, credit card, traveler's check 5.exercise
book, homework, pupil, teach 6.circular, rectangular, square, triangular

32 1.m 2.i 3.a 4.b 5.n 6.c 7.e 8.j 9.p 10.h 11.g 12.o 13.f 14.l 15.d 16.k

33 1.asleep 2.interesting 3.expensive 4.dark 5.empty 6.light 7.early 8.short 9.young
10.absent 11.noisy 12.happy 13.dangerous 14.hard 15.fat 16.strong

34 Set 1 1.g 2.b 3.i 4.j 5.a 6.c 7.f 8.e 9.d 10.h   Set 2 1.i 2.j 3.h 4.g 5.c 6.e 7.d 8.f 9.a 10.b

35 (For word square, see below page 96.) 1. 1.found out 2.made up 3.grew up 4.broke
down 5.got up 6.kept on 7.took off 8.heard from 2. 1.threw away 2.ran into 3.gave up
4.put off 5.sent for 6.thought over 7.blew up 8.cut off

36 1.accountant 2.astronomer 3.beggar 4.broadcaster 5.cyclist 6.director 7.gambler
8.winner 9.inhabitant 10.kidnapper 11.lawyer 12.leader 13.millionaire 14.novelist
15.receptionist 16.smuggler 17.specialist 18.voter

37 1.i 2.b 3.m 4.c 5.d 6.a 7.f 8.g 9.f 10.l 11.h 12.b 13.k 14.j 15.n 16.e
1.doggie bag 2.pot luck 3.happy hour 4.TV dinner

38 1.comfortable 2.dangerous 3.dirty 4.famous 5.foggy 6.hungry 7.icy 8.juicy 9.national
10.noisy 11.painful 12.powerful 13.rainy 14.sleepy 15.southern 16.successful 17.sunny
18.weekly 19.wonderful 20.wooden

39 1.forget 2.square 3.see 4.span 5.sound 6.simple 7.bone 8.clear 9.well 10.order

40 1.c 2.b 3.d 4.a 5.d 6.b 7.d 8.c 9.b 10.a 11.d 12.b 13.d 14.a 15.c 16.a

41 1.g 2.f 3.b 4.o 5.c 6.l 7.i 8.j 9.k 10.a 11.p 12.e 13.h 14.n 15.m 16.d

42 1.c 2.b 3.d 4.a 5.d 6.b 7.c 8.b 9.a 10.c 11.b 12.c 13.b 14.a

43 1.catch 2.teeth 3.earth 4.cloth 5.watch 6.death 7.rough 8.cough 9.match

44 1.h 2.k 3.i 4.j 5.c 6.l 7.e 8.f 9.d 10.g 11.b 12.a

45 1.e (florist) 2.d (optician's) 3.j (doctor's) 4.i (hotel) 5.f (bank) 6.c (theater)
7.b (barber's) 8.a (post office) 9.g (dentist's) 10.h (butcher's)

46 A Bear, pear, tear, wear. Dear, fear, gear, hear, near, rear, tear, year (also pronounced to rhyme with 'sir') **B** Chemistry, ache, character, echo, mechanic, scheme, school. Chair, bachelor, branch, change, cheese, check, chimney, choose, each, exchange, handkerchief **C** Girl, again, begin, get, gift, magazine, sugar, together. Age, general, generous, giant, gymnastics, magic, margarine, passenger

47 (For word square, see below page 96.) **A** 1.went out 2.carried on 3.brought up 4.did without 5.read through 6.left out 7.came across 8.stood out **B** 1.held up 2.set out 3.sold out 4.fell for 5.set off 6.hung up 7.wore out 8.caught up

48 1.l 2.k 3.e 4.g 5.a 6.f 7.c 8.b 9.n 10.j 11.d 12.h 13.i 14.m

49 1.Would you like to come to my party? 2.Would you like some more tea? 3.Would you like to borrow my calculator? 4.Would you like me to carry it? 5.Would you like me to teach you? 6.Let's go to a Chinese restaurant. 7.Let's stay at home. 8.Let's rent a video. 9.Let's go for a swim. 10.Let's take a taxi. 11.You'd better put on your raincoat. 12.You'd better call the dentist. 13.You'd better phone the police. 14.You'd better learn quickly. 15.You'd better call reception.

50 1.mad at 2.close to 3.good at 4.tired of 5.full of 6.similar to 7.anxious to 8.famous for 9.afraid of 10.grateful for 11.ready for 12.sorry for

51 1.stove,burner 2.bicycle,seat 3.piano,keys 4.clock,hand 5.shoe,heel 6.jacket,sleeve 7.telephone,receiver 8.dog,tail 9.boat,sails

52 1.big 2.lend 3.bring 4.buy 5.check 6.come 7.cook 8.floor 9.left 10.listen 11.tall 12.its 13.latest 14.passed 15.quiet 16.watched 17.tell 18.Whose

53 prime time, sitcom, soap opera, talk show; barbecue, deli, donut, dip; ballot, campaign, constituency, platform; dime, nickel, penny, quarter; ballad, jingle, lullaby, oldies; flabby, out of shape, sit-ups, sweats

54 1.j 2.h 3.b 4.a 5.g 6.n 7.e 8.k 9.l 10.f 11.c 12.m 13.i 14.d

55 1.crash helmet 2.goggles 3.coat 4.shirt 5.tie 6.necklace 7.pullover 8.belt 9.zipper 10.sock 11.shoe 12.boot 13.umbrella 14.glove 15.brooch 16.crown

56 Set 1 1.b 2.i 3.h 4.c 5.g 6.e 7.a 8.j 9.f 10.d   Set 2 1.g 2.a 3.f 4.j 5.c 6.b 7.h 8.d 9.e 10.i

57 1.rhinoceros 2.mouse 3.elephant 4.ostrich 5.bear 6.crab 7.giraffe 8.frog 9.penguin 10.owl 11.lion 12.crocodile

58 1.help 2.tried 3.carefully 4.hid 5.building 6.big 7.often 8.asked 9.needs 10.answer 11.looking 12.choose 13.fast/quickly 14. rich

59 1.shelf 2.faucet 3.sink 4.teapot 5.dish towel 6.pot 7.mixer 8.oven 9.stove 10.tablecloth 11.pitcher 12.bowl

60 1.accommodation 2.collection 3.comparison 4.complaint 5.composition 6.demonstration 7.difficulty 8.identification 9.illness 10.marriage 11.mixture 12.occupation 13.permission 14.punctuation 15.reservation 16.statement 17.suggestion 18.translation 19.treatment 20.weight

61 1.i 2.o 3.f 4.m 5.b 6.c 7.l 8.d 9.n 10.g 11.h 12.j 13.e 14.a 15.p 16.k 1.luggage rack 2.department store 3.word processor 4.orange juice

62 1.c 2.g 3.p 4.j 5.b 6.l 7.h 8.n 9.e 10.o 11.i 12.d 13.f 14.a 15.k 16.m
Pictures: 16.m, 8.n, 15.k, 14.a.

63 1.c 2.f 3.g 4.e 5.a 6.h 7.d 8.b

64 Set 1 1.c 2.e 3.i 4.h 5.a 6.j 7.f 8.d 9.b 10.g   **Set 2** 1.g 2.d 3.j 4.h 5.a 6.f 7.e 8.c 9.b 10i

65 1.passionate 2.cloudy 3.dusty 4.foolish 5.helpful 6.lucky 7.luxurious 8.medical 9.muddy 10.mysterious 11.nervous 12.original 13.personal 14.professional 15.reasonable 16.sensible 17.shiny 18.sympathetic 19. various 20.windy

66 1.marmalade 2.sheet 3.medicine 4.coffee 5.shampoo 6.newspaper 7.pants 8.film 9.socks 10.paint 11.television 12.bookcase 13.kettle 14.ring 15.watch

67 1.advise 2.delayed 3.invented 4.expect 5.suit 6.stranger 7.game 8.hard 9.job 10.lie 11.nearest 12.note 13.notice 14.took 15.prize 16.remind 17.road 18.stole

68 1.shark 2.monkey 3.zebra 4.rabbit 5.snake 6.bull 7.deer 8.horse 9.squirrel 10.pig 11.tortoise 12.parrot

69 1.sun 2.painting/picture 3.(tele)phone 4.knife 5.wind 6.(foot)ball 7.snow 8.tooth 9.passport 10.train 11.camera 12.library 13.dictionary 14.television

70 1.e 2.b 3.i 4.g 5.p 6.j 7.o 8.a 9.d 10.f 11.k 12.m 13.n 14.l 15.c 16.h
1.homework 2.freeway 3.sofa bed 4.postcard

71 1.g 2.m 3.h 4.d 5.o 6.l 7.k 8.a 9.f 10.p 11.j 12.i 13.n 14.e 15.b 16.c
Pictures: 6.l, 13.n, 11.j, 4.d

72 (For word square see below page 96.) 1.unusual 2.independent 3.untied 4.unable 5.incorrect 6.impossible

73 1.e 2.m 3.g 4.c 5.n 6.j 7.a 8.k 9.f 10.l 11.i 12.b 13.d. 14.h

74 1.j 2.g 3.i 4.a 5.h 6.b 7.e 8.f 9.d 10.c 11.Not right now, thanks. 12.Not me! 13.Not really. 14.Not very much. 15.Not very many.

Test 1	1.d	2.d	3.a	4.c	5.d	6.c	7.c	8.b	9.d	10.d	11.c	12.c	13.a	14.c	15.c
Test 2	1.d	2.d	3.d	4.d	5.a	6.c	7.d	8.b	9.a	10.c	11.d	12.b	13.c	14.d	15.c
Test 3	1.a	2.d	3.d	4.c	5.b	6.d	7.d	8.d	9.b	10.c	11.c	12.b	13.b	14.b	15.a
Test 4	1.c	2.b	3.c	4.b	5.a	6.b	7.d	8.b	9.c	10.d	11.b	12.d	13.b	14.d	15.d
Test 5	1.d	2.c	3.a	4.a	5.b	6.d	7.a	8.d	9.c	10.c	11.c	12.c	13.b	14a	15.d

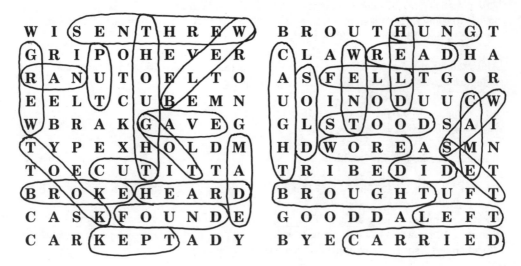

```
W I S E N T H R E W      B R O U T H U N G T
G R I P O H E V E R      C L A W R E A D H A
R A N U T O E L T O      A S F E L L T G O R
E E L T C U B E M N      U O I N O D U U C W
W B R A K G A V E G      G L S T O O D S A I
T Y P E X H O L D M      H D W O R E A S M N
T O E C U T I T T A      T R I B E D I D E T
B R O K E H E A R D      B R O U G H T U F T
C A S K F O U N D E      G O O D D A L E F T
C A R K E P T A D Y      B Y E C A R R I E D
```

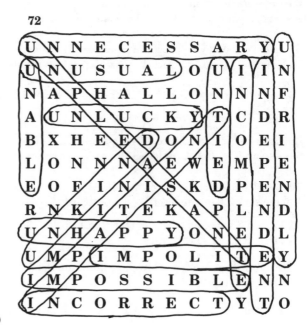

```
U N N E C E S S A R Y U
U N U S U A L O U I I N
N A P H A L L O N N N F
A U N L U C K Y T C D R
B X H E E D O N I O E I
L O N N N A E W E M P E
E O E I N I S K D P E N
R N K I T E K A P L N D
U N H A P P Y O N E D L
U M P I M P O L I T E Y
I M P O S S I B L E N N
I N C O R R E C T Y T O
```

(In fact, there are 15 adjectives !)